BUSING TO BYZANTIUM

Selected Poems and Prose

by

Bruce Guernsey

D0814406

For my dear wife Victoria,

Shaper of hearts and gems,

And in memory of my sister Dawn,

Whose wit, no matter the night,

Lit every morning.

© 2021 by Bruce Guernsey

Published by Pine Row Press
107 W Orchard Road
Ft. Mitchell, KY 41011

ISBN: 978-1-7363394-0-4

March 2021

First Edition

10 9 8 7 6 5 4 3 2 1

Cover photo credit:
Omer Tohma from "Unsplash," Istanbul

Publisher's website at pinerow.com

Author's website at bruceguernsey.com

BUSING TO BYZANTIUM

THE WELL

The mystery of water underground,
the dark stream where the dead kneel
cupping their pale hands,
splashing the stillness from their eyes.

I drop a stone in ours to hear
if there's water for the children's bath.
And if it's dry, no sound—the pebble
a star, falling through the night.

Here, a rope once hung, a bucket
on its noose. Here, the cattle gathered
summer evenings at the trough,
their dull heads bowed.

No one fishes this hole, or ever did,
though in the cold, moonless pools
fins move through the dark, deep
in the ground, where spawning begins.

FROM RAIN

Around Easter
when the woods are still pastel
and the air is damp with April,
I need to feel the river's pull
I haven't felt all winter,

this longing I have for water
that leads me here where cutbanks swell
with spring from every hill,
mysterious, maternal,
and into that fullness I enter,

myself no longer
but one with the shifting gravel,
and, like these mayflies hatching in swirls,
from rain I've come, will spinning fall
as once and ever,

both son and father,
eternal and ephemeral
while the current around me curls
and I lift my line in this ritual
of rod and river, of Adam and lover.

-- for Victoria

JANUARY THAW

This is the time of forgiveness,
when your father
would bend down to you
just before sleep,
the breath of his kiss
the warmth of this breeze
as you walk the slope
behind the house,
the land you'd forgotten
under the drifts:
how the stones,
steaming with light,
steady the earth
in the melting snow.

THE RAVEN'S GIFT

I am sitting in a one-bedroom cabin made of spruce logs and heated by small chunks of birch I split in the brief light of yesterday afternoon. It is mid-December and light is diminishing everywhere in the northern hemisphere, but here, sixteen miles northeast of Fairbanks, Alaska, light is like the grapefruit I bought a few days ago: rare and precious and something you crave no matter the cost. "Who cares how expensive they are," my friend Nancy said as we pushed a cart through the produce section at the giant Fred Myers store in town. "When I first moved here twenty years ago, I didn't even like grapefruit," she laughed. "Now look." She was loading our cart with them, with some oranges and apples, too, and I was amazed at the selection of fresh fruit in the store, this far north and this time of year. But it was that big yellow fruit that people were drawn to the most, to pick up and hold.

"They remind me the sun is shining somewhere, somewhere way south of here," Nancy said, as we drove back in the dark along the Chena Hot Springs Road. "They cheer me up." And now that I've been this far north for a few days myself, I've begun to understand that symbolism. A grapefruit is the sun itself in your hand—the same sun that now makes its low, horizontal way from southeast to southwest, six minutes more quickly each day until by the twenty-first of this last month of the year, there will be only three hours and forty-two minutes of daylight.

Today, the sixteenth of December, it's twenty below, the coldest day so far of my winter solstice experiment to live alone in the dark. And dark it is, even at 8:25 AM on the cabin's pendulum clock, its steady heartbeat my only company. There's usually little wind in central Alaska during the winter, something I was glad to learn, because the kind of wind that I'm used to on the plains of Illinois would make this still world impossible to survive. Wind would tear at its

11

beauty, too, as the snow, feathery-dry, balances on the branches of spruce so delicately that the wing-beat of a chickadee will set it adrift.

The lightness of this snow has been one of my most important discoveries in the long walks I've taken on the sled dog trails nearby my cabin. The snow that hovers so precariously on boughs beside the paths I puff along is far different than that packed hard by the traffic of mushers. When there's sun enough to see my way, I follow the tracks of their wooden runners, and sometimes through the thin air, can hear the dogs far off in front of me. Or are they somewhere behind? Who can tell in this immensity of wilderness?—their distant howl reminding me of the hoot of the train that brought my father home from work in the twilight when I was a boy growing up in the suburbs. I'd wait by the door, peering through the mail slot, searching the shadows for his brisk stride up our walk. I wanted him home, though he seldom was, working late to support six kids.

There I go again: so easily linking a moment in the present with some loneliness in my past. Sadness is a deep part of me. Its ache is forever there in my chest, a fact that I have come to accept over time and no longer dwell on its sources. "In a dark time/ the eye begins to see," wrote the poet, Theodore Roethke, and I have come to Alaska this darkest of months to find where light might be in such a time, in such a place. A century ago, prospectors by the thousands made their way here, digging and sifting the landscape, rubbing off the dirt to find what gleams underneath. I am doing the same.

"It's not the cold that gets to [many Alaskans] in the winter, it's the darkness," writes Susan Ewing in her informative guide, *The Great Alaska Nature Fact Book*. The effect of reduced sunlight—called SAD, for "seasonal affective disorder"—is apathy and depression, most probably brought about by increased levels of the hormone melatonin in the bloodstream as the days grow shorter. One remedy is sitting under a lamp that imitates nature's big one. Perhaps eating grapefruit is another.

Or maybe celebrating the snow itself: "winter's silver lining," as Ewing calls it. Snowfalls come in all shapes and sizes up here. For example, Barrow, the northernmost town, gets only a couple of feet, whereas Valdez on Prince William Sound gets the whole nine yards—twenty-seven feet of "the white stuff," the cliché of weathermen in the lower States. But as Susan Ewing informs us, there are some two hundred words in Eskimo dialects to describe what I have found here in central Alaska: snow as luminous as mica and nothing like the hardened stuff of winter thoroughfares back home. Instead, it graces the limbs beside the paths and reflects the first light of the late morning. Weightless and shimmering, this whiteness that's settled on the branches leads me along the trails.

The snow has also given me a kind of reading material. Fortunately, the print is large and easy to see in the dim light.

There are the footprints of the hare, for example, nicknamed "snowshoe" for its hind feet, which are so large that they land in front of its front ones when it's hopping. These giant bunnies are plentiful every ten years, and I must be here at the height of their cycle. I see their tracks newly printed each day, together with fresh ones of their mortal enemy, the lynx, its broad, soft paws like letterpress on the white page of this "book to be read," as Alaska's best poet, John Haines, has described the snow. And most obvious of all, and yet most mysterious, is the wide, rounded contour of a moose where it slept in the last twenty-four hours, now vanished. But where, I wonder? And how?—that shambling, awkward moose. How could something so huge just disappear? I look about, stare into the vastness, but see nothing.

Because the sun never gets high enough, its rays can't penetrate to where I walk below. Instead, they run parallel to the ground, making candles of the snowy tops of spruce I look up to, penitent and believing. It's like being in a gothic cathedral, in the nave at Chartres perhaps, where the lofty columns lift your gaze to the brilliant light above, high up and holy through the stained glass. Here, too, I want to genuflect at the fire that burns at the top of these towering evergreens, but to keep from freezing, must mush myself along instead, glancing up as I go, the thick rubber of my boots squeaking irreverently through the stillness.

But not, perhaps, as irreverent as the ravens that perch, puff, and palaver on the branches as I walk. They seem to be talking to one another, probably something about that wandering human down there. "Ke-dowk," jokes one; "ko-wulk-ulk-ulk," chuckles the other. Or so Susan Ewing tries to quote them, these iridescent intellectuals who speak more than sing. Poe's literary version has only one word it says, the famous "Nevermore," which is but three syllables compared to the five that these real birds can make, plus all kinds of inflections.

Ravens also mate for life, something the poet probably didn't know. That these birds are together for twenty years or more adds a real poignancy to Poe's bookish poem about the loss of the lovely Lenore. Single now myself, I'm a little envious of these special creatures. When I see a pair of them, I think of some old couple chatting away on their park-bench limb, descendants both of "Dat-soon-sah," the Great Raven of Athabascan myth who created the world. Its gift was light. Black as night, the Great Raven brought us day.

Yesterday, the weather warmed to minus fifteen, so I hiked a little farther out and emerged from the dark green boughs that line the trail into a whole forest of birch, white as the snow. The sight was dazzling and made me squint, like coming out of a matinee into the bright sunshine. I'd stepped into perfect light, not a spruce anywhere, and each trunk long and lithe, not one bent by ice storm or some playful boy climbing to the top and swinging down, as Robert Frost imagines in his poem, "Birches." Pure plumblines of light seemingly dropped from the sky, these trees lit the winter twilight on their own.

The pamphlet about trees I bought in town tells me some things about the birch I didn't know. As a boy summering in New Hampshire, I called them simply "white birch," a kind of generic name. But the proper name is "paper birch," and I would use it that way, peeling off long strips and writing secret notes to hide in the stone walls, messages to the chipmunks and trolls. "Betula papyrifera," the family and genus, makes me realize that others, thousands of years ago, recognized the same thing: that like papyrus, a scroll from this tree can hold our secrets or be our letter to the world.

"Birch" comes from the Old English word, "beorht," meaning "bright," and in Sanscrit, "bhrajate," the probable genesis of both words, means "to shine." "Spirit lights," the Inuit people call the more famous Aurora Borealis, but I wonder if they have a name for these remarkable birch forests which to me are as mysterious as those billowing pale greens and pinks I've seen several nights in a row. I've watched them change their shape like wraiths and suddenly vanish. They deserve their fame on post cards and in the slick photographic books on sale everywhere in Fairbanks. People come from all over the world this time of year to witness this incandescence, young Japanese couples especially who believe that soaking together under the northern lights at Chena Hot Springs will increase their fertility.

Stands of birch have no such legends about them, having none of that cosmic energy. But from energy they have come: many of these groves are the result of fire from lightning that seared the land and have risen phoenix-like across this wilderness. And energy they now give out: the light from these trees—dozens and dozens of them, some up to eighty feet tall—enough to make even the most unpoetic mind believe with Frost that "earth's the right place for love."

But sometimes it is not, and like the poet, I have found that "I'd like to get away from earth awhile," and once tried to do so for real. I was in Greece and sunlight was everywhere that April morning, but I didn't notice. Hurt by love, I simply did not wish to be. So, I stepped out into the traffic, into the frenzy of honking and tires squealing that suddenly became as silent as it is here. The inner calm I felt at that moment I had never experienced before, nor have I since. "Death, death, death, death," Walt Whitman heard inside him as he walked along the shore as a child, "the low and delicious word death," and now I'd heard it, too, and found it as soothing.

Good thing the Greeks are such inventive drivers, dodging one another on the road, because I made it to the other side where I heard the horns again, the tires, and the word "malaka" from the irate cabbies who had saved my life, though they didn't know it. To them I was just another masturbating loser (a rough translation of "malaka"), and perhaps I was, so self-involved as to try to kill myself. But the peace I felt, that peace—what a lure it was.

Despite my Catholic upbringing, I have learned that hell is not a place, anymore than heaven is. Greece and Alaska: literally day and night, but the inferno was within me then, many years ago, and it didn't matter what my melatonin level was, there in sunny Greece. And here I am now finding something holy in this darkened world where the moisture in my nose freezes instantly when I step outside and where my beard has become a brilliant spider web of ice when I come back in after my walk. "Hoarfrost," that's called, when the air's simply too cold to hold any moisture and so water vapor condenses onto any surface it can find, like windows or my face. For a frozen moment I am Tennyson or Whitman with their flowing, frosty beards of wisdom. Or perhaps Santa Claus, who also finds joy in dark December and this far north.

I'm not much of a fan of Christmas lights, but my experience here has taken me back to a time when those lights meant something. The chamber of commerce in my home town actually awards prizes to the most garish displays of illuminated rooftops, plastic reindeer, and Jesus-in-neon. Sadly, my community, like much of the country, has come to celebrate style over substance, the fate of every tradition once its origin is forgotten, which seems to be the case, I hear, in the shabby town of North Pole, south of Fairbanks on the Richardson Highway.

There you have "Santa Claus Lane," full of all the ornamental trappings of the solstice. What a shame, because Nancy tells me that such tawdry displays are rare. Instead, I have witnessed their pagan genesis: the very darkness itself and set against it, a simple string of tiny lights perhaps, candle-like around a doorway. Nothing fancy, nothing showy. That's because encounter here is actual; the cold will kill. What a symbol it is, that solitary light along an empty roadway. "We are here," it says. "We are alive."

This indelible image of the single, simple light must account for the importance of the roadhouse in Alaskan history. There are not many of them left, alas. Holiday Inns and other such corporate giants have moved here, too, and their neon signs, together with the false gold of McDonalds' arches, ignite the night sky in downtown Fairbanks to white out the stars and northern lights. In the base camp town of Talkeetna, however, and at the junction of the Richardson and Denali Highways, the roadhouse truly keeps the porch light on for you, not just the empty words of a television commercial. Since most travel before the car and plane occurred in winter, the roadhouse would provide a modest bed and board to dog-sled teams who must have seen its warmth from far off, just as the modern traveler to central Alaska in December can glimpse from the jet's window a moment of light in all that dark: someone's homestead down there and nothing else but wilderness near.

But off in the distance, down the snowbound dirt road that leads to that home, what's this, making its slow way through the afternoon night? The school bus! That land-bound bush plane with its treasure from Fairbanks, the light on its roof flickering and flashing. When I see one lumber along the Hot Springs Road, turn and disappear into the tunnel of some unmarked lane, I become a young parent again, checking my watch, worried the bus is ten minutes late. Black ice, a dead battery: anything could happen this time of year. And then to see it come over the hill—oh, yellow, yellow, home safe is the school bus! The color of daffodils, it melts the dark no matter how cold.

It's time to stoke the stove. I open the firebox slowly, stir the coals and lay in some kindling: branches, sticks, and any chips from yesterday's splitting that I brought inside. Next, I stack the smaller logs, carefully at an angle to let the fire breathe as I blow, then I take a deep breath and blow again until we seem to be breathing together, the fire and I— the heat, the glow, now part of me: this glowing heat, the raven's gift.

"Thank you, my night-feathered friends," I say aloud, and kneeling, roll a big log on as the sun comes up, touching with light the wicks of the trees.

NORTH

Up here, in this cold,
you won't get fat.

I don't mean your ribs,
I mean your words.

Far north, in the deep snow,
nouns are skin and bone

for verbs to gnaw on,
lean as ice, raw as oak—

cut, clear; split, burn—
one breath, one bite

up here where *ax*
is both a thing and work.

THE COMPASS

Each fall with a stone
I drive a stake
by the well in our yard,

a hardwood pole
chiseled sharp
I stab in the earth's

cold heart—
a steady point
in the blowing white

where tracks fill fast
and sleep comes on
like finding home.

SOMETIMES FOR HOURS

At my feet my dog,
a pastoral scene,

master and beast,
except in his dream

he's chasing a car,
flinching awake

as the wheels hit—
the way we do

falling through sleep,
suddenly saved.

What the mind questions,
the heart believes

and we lie there reasoning,
afraid.

The dog instead
scratches his ear,

nips at a flea
and is soon back twitching.

But we,
we lie in the night

sometimes for hours
wondering

why the lights
that cross the ceiling

from a passing car
trouble us so,

a moment of light
in all that dark.

DOUBLEMINT

"Chew Doublemint: it cleans your teeth and breath," Gene Autry used to tell us at the end of his show on Sunday nights. He'd just emptied his six-shooter into some scruffy bad guy and had rid the town of evil, but my favorite cowboy's dental advice had little effect on my mother. "No," was all she had to say, which meant in no uncertain terms, no gum for me, despite my pleading at the grocery store.

The memory of tugging at my mother's sleeve came forcefully back to me last year on the streets of Ho Chi Minh City when a rag doll of a child, this unwashed little girl, kept tugging at my shirt with her dirty hand, a green pack of clean-Gene's version of toothpaste in the other. "Don't buy it," John said. "If you do, she's yours for life." Little did I know at the time how true those words would be.

John is John Balaban, a good friend now, but then my experienced guide around the city where I'd arrived as a faculty member with Semester-at-Sea, a unique program of worldwide travel and shipboard study. Vietnam was our fourth port of call, and Balaban had joined us in Hong Kong, our previous landing, as an interport lecturer. This was one of his many visits to the country. A specialist in Vietnamese culture, he'd been a conscientious objector during the war, courageously helping to find medical care for napalmed children.

"No," I told her, taking his advice and echoing my mother, but this kid with the smudged face was more daring and persistent than I was at her age. I kept thinking that had she a mother like mine to swat her bottom, she wouldn't keep after me this way, buzzing about like a fly. "Mister, mister," I heard wherever I turned, but I didn't give in.

That night, back in the safety of our ship, the SS Universe Explorer—nicknamed "The Great White Mother"—I heard similar tales from my colleagues about street children like "Double," as I had come to call my tenacious shadow by the end of the day. Over drinks and dinner, Balaban explained to us that these kids had no certain set of parents and were essentially homeless. "They do look out for one another," he

31

went on to say. "A kind of extended family," but he warned that we'd continue something that had gone on since the war by buying the candy and gum they had to sell.

Later, in the snug of my cabin, I was struck by the pathos of a child trying to market the very sweets most kids beg for as I had. Thank goodness she vanished, I thought, but falling asleep, I saw her again, her thin, oversized dress slipping into the crowd outside the fence at the dock. Giving in to my guilt would be good for me, not her, I kept saying to myself like a bedtime prayer. Balaban is right and so was my old lady. And what would the equivalent of twenty-five cents really mean out there anyway? Yes, it's a good thing she's gone, but where I wondered, where?

I didn't sleep well that night. Dreams are the soul's home movies, someone once said, and somehow home and TV and images of the "American" war, as the Vietnamese call it, all got confused in my head. The next morning, at the old American Embassy where I'd gone with Balaban to take some pictures, was I sleeping or awake? Everywhere litter was blowing about, bits of paper and shredded strips of palm leaves from the whirring blades overhead, the chopper lifting, desperate hands reaching, trying to grab on, then falling back to ground, wailing faces wedged in the bars of the locked iron gate.

I stood now at that very place and it all came back to me: the last days of the war, the horror of that evacuation that I watched with my fellow Americans in our living rooms as our country abandoned the many thousands of South Vietnamese who would surely die. The Embassy was sealed off still but hardly regal now, overgrown and falling in.

"Mister, mister," I heard in my waking dream, and even John was amazed. How she found us I have no idea any more than I could explain how a lost dog finds its way home. Was she even the same child, I wondered, because today her hair was combed and her hands washed as if she were meeting someone special. She wore the same long dress, however: a gossamer hand-me-down from who-knows-whom that made her look even smaller and younger than the eight or nine she probably was—that made her look almost transparent, more wraith than flesh. But in her fist there was the pack of Doublemint. She was back, and she was real.

By the end of the day, I finally gave in. Balaban, my version of Virgil, had gone into a shop and the little girl and I were alone. "Listen," I said to her as if she could understand, "if I buy some gum will you go away?" Resisting her salesmanship hadn't worked, so I thought I'd try the other, though something inside of me kept saying, no, no. But what was this voice saying "no" to, I wondered—to buying the gum or having her leave? "No, no, please don't, don't go," yet who was saying this, her or me?

I offered John a stick of gum when he came out. I thought he'd be miffed, especially when I told him about the extra quarter I'd given her for a tip, but he, too, seemed to admire her incredible persistence and maybe even missed having her around the way I did on our way back to the ship. While watching for pickpockets and dodging motor scooters, I couldn't help but search the twilight for my small friend, but like any shadow at dusk, she was nowhere to be seen. Was she only after my money, little as I gave her? I was strangely sad, felt somehow abandoned, and spent the evening with my children who were students on board.

They were wisely not taking any of my courses, but I wanted them to know about a Vietnamese story I'd just taught called "The Key" by Vo Phien. It deals with a family's having to leave behind a very old and feeble grandfather during the hurried evacuation. In that frenzy, the narrator forgot to leave a key for the old man who is his father, to open a trunk where his valuables are stored. Having made it safely to America with wife and children, the narrator wears the key around his neck like a cross. No matter where he goes, even in the refugee shower where he tells his tale like a penance, he wears that key, opening his heart to all who will listen.

The Vietnamese have a deep tradition of ancestor worship. Despite how he cleaned himself in that hot, steamy water, the voice in Vo Phien's touching story can never wash away his memories. I couldn't get "Double" out of my mind either, and vowed the next day, after I visited the market, to find her. I'll buy every pack of gum that kid has, by God. Every stick of the stuff.

I happen to love markets and go to them each time I visit a new country. Some people claim that to know a culture, study their burial rights. I say instead, go to where they live, to the place they buy their food: to where the colors delight and the smells arouse, or don't. Then you'll discover through your senses who these people are. My visit to this particular one made me realize, even more, how little we knew, and know, about the Vietnamese.

Arranged with the wonder of a child's eye, the central market place in Ho Chi Minh City is a coloring book of lively lemons and purple dragon fruit piled high against an orange sky, a dazzle of line and light. Wandering the web of aisles, it didn't take long for me to lose myself in vast deserts of rice, tinged nut-brown to angel-white in dunes the size of pyramids. The aquarium I kept as a kid never swam with the motion of the fish in the chilly stalls I came upon, silver-pink and moony-gold on beds of ice where tiger prawns the length of lobsters still crawled a coral reef.

I think I bought one of each, of the fruit at least. Stepping out into the hoots and horns of the city reminded me of leaving the shelter of the Saturday matinee, still dreamy, still riding with my heroes like Gene Autry in the latest western and rubbing my eyes at the light. The traffic soon brought me back to my mission, and I hired a cyclo to take me around town. A shadow needs to eat, I said to myself: good thing you bought all that fruit. It's bound to spoil, so you'd better find her.

A cyclo ride is exciting. The driver, the Vietnamese version of a gondolier, sits behind and slightly above his passenger, peddling deftly around the city's many flowered circles: a scary but aesthetic experience as carts and wagons, trucks and cars, merge with the flashing spokes of spinning wheels, meshing together in a myriad of colors. It's like being inside a kaleidoscope.

Bags of fruit for company, I rode my hired tricycle wherever I pointed, much to the confusion of the driver in his cone-shaped straw hat. "Where go?" he wanted to know, but I had no answer, other than to wave my hand like a wand, hoping my missing friend would magically appear. "There was a girl," I finally tried to explain, almost an hour later, and he nodded his head. "Girl," he understood, and we took a right down a side-street I'd not yet seen, to a bar where the hanging beads for a door swayed softly, seductively.

Sorrow came upon me in a rush. This, of course, is where she might someday be but not with gum to clean your teeth and breath. At that moment there was nothing more I wanted in the world than "clean," nothing more than to be a kid again, riding his trike down the block, but even the fruit beside me seemed to leer up luridly. "The zoo," I blurted out, "take me to the zoo." That's where kids go, and opening my map, I found the city gardens.

I paid him well, my driver, who departed shaking his head, confused by my lack of direction, baffled perhaps by my manhood. "Girls" were undoubtedly one of his typical fares, but what could he think of some lost guy interested in monkeys and elephants? And a humble zoo it was besides. I bought some peanuts to feed the sad-faced pachyderm that came snuffling toward me, its face full of flies. A group of small children all in school uniform came by, but "Double," of course, was not among them. Some older girls, too, in their late teens, wearing the emblems of their status: traditional white blouses, silky-long over their flowing pants, so beautiful.

How ironic, I thought—no, how sad—that the same word in Vietnamese for "America" is this very one, "beautiful." I almost tried to say it—"mehi," or something like that, as I'd learned from John Balaban—so lovely were these young women before me, in procession like they were going to communion, but the chattering of monkeys woke me from my wanderings, and I made my empty way back to the "Great White Mother," needing the warmth of her sheltering arms but realizing at the same time how privileged we all were in her protectiveness. The ship was always there to welcome us back, to feed and tuck us in, her motion a cradle, forever rocking.

We set sail the next morning early, long before anybody might be at the gate to wave goodbye. I waved back anyway, climbing to the top deck at sunrise, a symbolic gesture to a country I'd first known as a time, not a place; not a country at all, in fact, but a war I'd done my best to stay out of. White and well-educated, I had learned how to use the deferment system. I was lucky in the draft lottery, too, where to come in last was to win. But having now finally been to this haunted land, it was time to rethink what was lost or won. "If you do, she's yours for life." Balaban's words still echo. How did he know? Could it be that he, too, walked hand-in-hand with the same little girl? Is that why he keeps returning? Is this what he meant?

Fortunately, busy work with classes kept me busy. For a while, at least. My shadow still hid in the dark and tugged at my sleeve again a few days later out at sea. Some students I hadn't thought much of, the giggly and studly types, told in our daily "core" class of something they'd done in Vietnam. We were all required to attend these general meetings which were often a drag, but not this one.

"She was like such a mess, this little girl. I mean, she was like, you know, dirty." I was stunned at what I was hearing. So that's where she was, my Doublemint! These students, as they went on to tell us, had taken her out to buy some clothes. Amazing! Out of all those thousands of children on the streets, they'd dressed her up that last day. I felt relieved. No wonder we couldn't find each other: she was with them, being cared for, I at that moment believed.

And part of me still does. After all, as I was warned, she's mine for life, just like the country she'd come to mean.

THE DUMP PICKERS

On Sundays
carting my trash to the dump
I'd see them swarming
the piles like gnats,
a whole family of pickers
straight from Mass:
Dad's suit, white
as the noon sky, Junior
in a polka-dot tie—
in bright, patent leathers
his small, pale sister.

From the highest of piles
Mother shouted orders
through a paper cup,
the men hurrying under
her red, high heels,
dragging metal to the pickup,
the little girl giggling,
spinning on her toes
through the blowing paper
like a dancer, a little twist
of wind in the dust.

THE LADY AND THE TRAMP

As my mother's memory dims
she's losing her sense of smell
and can't remember the toast
blackening the kitchen with smoke
or sniff how nasty the breath of the dog
that follows her yet from room to room,
unable, himself, to hear his own bark.

It's thus they get around,
the wheezing old hound stone deaf
baying like a smoke alarm
for his amnesiac mistress whose back
from petting him is bent forever
as they shuffle towards the flaming toaster
and split the cindered crisp that's left.

HIGH FLYING

9/11/2001

In the living room
in his jump-seat
my son
hangs from the branch
of the door sill
asleep, a pilot
slumped in his parachute.

Unstrapping the limp,
vulnerable body
I lift him to bed
on the rough
stretcher of my arms—
easy, easy now—
as a medic the wounded.

He stirs once
to reassure me
and returns, weary
from a day
of high flying, of singing
so close to heaven,
unaware of the world's weight
and yet to learn
the brutal power of flight.

AMERICAN HARDWARE

Just lay your hardware on the table, cowboy,
and keep them hands up high.

Last Sunday I bumped into Ron at the hardware store. In the central mid-west where I live, it's not unusual to meet an old friend pushing his cart along full of home repairs, especially on a Sunday. True Value and Ace are to us what Starbucks is to those in the big city. There, it's espresso and croissants; here, WD 40 with a fresh roll of duct tape. The hardware store is also where everyone seems to go after church; or, more and more, instead of church, plaster replacing prayer on the Lord's Day.

Ron was coming down the aisle that I was headed up, neither of us looking where he was going, preoccupied. A pipe was leaking in my basement, and I was scanning the shelves for cement to help hold the plastic fittings tight. Something always needs fixing in a house, but after my divorce, the place I'd moved into seemed particularly fragile: holes in the roof, ripped screens, the plumbing gone sour. If a

45

man's home is his castle, mine was under siege, but the enemy was within. I had come to see the cliché about putting your life back together in terms of my house. Too bad there's no home-owner's insurance for sorrow, no "good hands" to be in but your own. Thus, patching this or that in the old place became a symbol of self-repair, and I'd started going to the local hardware religiously.

Ron was a former neighbor, the kind of guy who's good with tools and can fix most anything. Our wives had gotten along well and our kids were roughly the same age, so Ron and I had grilled a lot of chicken together, backyard evenings, over the years. He had also saved me both headaches and cash with his do-it-yourself handiwork. For whatever reasons that probably Freud could best explain, I never adopted my father's similar fix-it abilities. I'd turned to words instead of wood; to semi-colons, not nails.

We collided where plumbing meets electrical, both of us shocked back into the present from wherever we were, whoever it was. "Hey." "Howyabeen?" "I don't believe it."

46

"What's goin' on?"—the usual guy talk from two guys who hadn't seen each other in a couple of years. Seeing how you yourself have changed is next to impossible; that's what class reunions are for. "*He's* older, good thing I'm not," we say to ourselves as I did, looking at Ron as he stared at me. His burly, Polish shape was gone. "Ski" was skinny but not around the eyes where lines he never had before tugged them down. "Looks like you've lost some weight," he said, and I wondered which of us was talking.

We both were, just as we had tried to stay in touch after I had moved from town to the country three years back. A beer here, a beer there, then we gradually went our ways. When I'd heard that his wife was sick, I called and was pleased to hear she was doing better. "We'll beat this," he said. "Not much of a lump. We found it early." Same old Ron, still saying "we." No man loved his wife more. And there, too, was that old confidence I'd come to count on despite how horrible the house disaster he came over to fix and did. His attitude and strength were the same back then, a pipe wrench in his thick hand, as they were that time on the phone. If only we were all like houses, made of concrete or wood.

Doris died the following Christmas. I was out of the country when it happened but did send a card. Our meeting at American Hardware was the first chance I'd had to say "I'm sorry" in person, something I should have done months ago. Why hadn't I, I wondered, as we stood there talking about the Bears. Partly my own troubles, I'm sure, but a kind of shyness, too, an awkwardness with feelings. But another voice, a new one, more self-assured, had begun to emerge within me in the last few months—a voice that seemed to understand courage in a new way, to define strength differently. To the cowardly me it said: you're getting better at home repairs, now it's time to get better at the more demanding ones, the emotional kind.

Give this guy a hug, dammit!

I would have had to climb over our burdened carts to do so, and men embracing among electrical sockets and ball joints would have been a little more than this small town can handle, especially on a Sunday. Instead, we talked for almost an hour and not just about football or varieties of waterproof cement. Right there on the hardwood hardware floor, we got positively Emersonian, by God, talking self-reliance and what it was like to be alone. "I love my house, man. It keeps me going," and I told Ron I felt the same way. I'd come to like being my own carpenter and plumber. My father would have been proud. Amazed.

Not that either Ron or I had started subscribing to *House Beautiful* or anything. Our goals were hardly decorative nor were they simply practical. My old man had learned how to fix things because we were poor, though he certainly took pride in what he did. I could now afford to hire a plumber but chose not to because home repair had become self-repair as it had, I realized, for Ron. You could see it in the sadness of his eyes. I think he saw it, too, in mine.

The spiritual side of Emerson's notion of self-reliance has long since been replaced by sermons from Mount Hardware or salvation by Sears. But Ron and I were clearly in that store of edges and angles for more than just the old macho reasons, or the cheapo ones either. A couple of softies in a hard place, we were there precisely to make repairs but from the outside in. I want to believe that inside every John Wayne with his two-fisted syllables was the more vulnerable, Marion Morrison, his real, more lyrical name, but know that every day I have to duel it out with that part of me called "The Duke" just like many other American males have or will.

Give this man a hug, dammit.

Okay, here goes, and I tried, but Ron seemed to have the same idea, and we banged together like tackles and guards in a clatter of plastic elbows and dripless faucets we scattered from the shelves. From all over the store, people came running. What, they must have wondered aisles away, could have started all that laughing?

DOUG

When my father came home from the war
two years after I was born
I couldn't match his voice with his picture
and cried each time he came near.

Learning to talk, I called him "Doug,"
the way my mother did,
this strange man always trying to hold me—
how could he be my dad?

My father was there, right there in black and white
over my bed every morning
where I could see him with his uniform on,
boarding a train, waving good-by and smiling,

not that deep voice down the hall,
not those footsteps outside my door.
No, my dad's a soldier who'll be home soon,
so watch out you, whoever you are.

Then Doug went away like him,
leaving for work before dawn,
the knocker on the front door always tapping
as he closed it behind him in the dark,

the big brass knocker that brought me running
to peer through the mail slot
for him who never knocked, who never came,
only Doug, home late

each night from work, this man Doug
marching up the stairs, the hall light
fierce behind him in my doorway,
a blanket in his hand.

NIGHT PATROL

My father never slept real well after the war
and as my mother tells, he woke in fear
so deep, so far away, he seemed to stare
straight out at nothing she could see or hear.

Or worse—she wraps her robe around her, remembering—
he'd sit there grinning, bolt upright beside her,
this mad look on his face, the bed springs quivering
with some hilarity the night had whispered.

And once, "He did this your father, I swear he did—
he must have been still dreaming, rest his soul—
he tried to close my frightened eyes, my lids,
to thumb them shut like he was on patrol

the way he'd learned so they would sleep, the dead.
And then he blessed himself and bowed his head."

THE RITUAL

The first night of frost
we all have our chores,
the children in the garden
picking tomatoes
hard as apples;
in their mother's hands,
the final flowers.
I hood in plastic
what plants I can
and as the wind stills
lug in wood,
stacking oak against the dark
the clearest night of the year.

The first night of frost
we go to bed early,
the children at their prayers,
in the darkness
their soft words;
my wife in her slippers
going up the stairs.
I open the window
and smell the air,
hear as I hold her
in the warmth of our bed
a dog bark, far off,
under the stars.

UNCLES

"My father!—methinks I see my father."
--Hamlet

A few years ago, I became an uncle. I'd never been one before, just as I'd never been a father until my son was born, or a husband before I got married. I've always been a son, however—that's one role we can all count on, being a son or a daughter, and it's a role that each of us has to ad lib on our own. There's no clear script, and we make up the part as we go along.

But being a father or a mother?—we have some idea, most of us determined to do better, or at least as well, as our own parents and theirs before them and onward back. I'm not sure I'm ready to be a grandfather yet; there's too much time involved in that role: time gone by, that is. But an uncle? A kind of stepping-stone on the path to "granddad"? Yes, I'm all for that, perhaps because I had such wonderful and weird ones myself: four of them altogether, and each a very different person. Four surrogate fathers like fingers on the generational hand with my father the thumb: thumbs up, thumbs down, depending on how I did. My uncles, instead, were far less judgmental, yet all of them helped to point my way whether they knew it or not.

It's no great news to say that fathers and sons often have trouble communicating. This Freudian fact, combined with my father's lack of verbal skills and seeming uneasiness with affection, often led me to seek from one of my uncles what I thought was missing in him. Since Pop was always too busy to take me fishing, I'd go with his brother, Alfred, who did have the time because he couldn't hold a job for long. I loved to watch him cast, his fly line unrolling over the stream like the lyrical sweep of a swallow. Or, when my father acted mean, I turned to his daffy brother-in-law, my Uncle Donald, who convinced me by seven or eight that I could fly.

Alfred, Donald, and Charles, my father's youngest brother, had all been in the Second World War, as had my father. Its scars were deep. Only Sheldon, the oldest Guernsey brother, had not gone. The law at that time allowed first sons an exemption, and he had two children by then of his own. He still lived near the family farm in upstate New York, and when we'd go there from north Jersey each spring to visit and to bring home fryers for the freezer, I was the one sent into the hen house to grab a chicken for the chopping block. After all, I was nine, and this was one of those gauntlets I had to run as a boy.

Road Island Reds, the squawking hens were: big, heavy birds that when I reached for one, beat the top of my head with its violent flapping and spurred my wrists until they bled. Like Abraham, my father raised his hatchet as I knelt by the block, holding the thrashing bird as best I could, its eyes bead-red with fear then suddenly closed for good by the blue, translucent lids on the head beside me in the dust. My father would throw the body in the air, and it would somehow land on its feet to run about spouting blood in a frighteningly comical panic as if some unseen hawk were hovering above.

I couldn't eat eggs or chicken for years, not with that startling sight in my dreams and the indelible smell of wet yellow fat on my hands, globs of it among the scalded feathers as I plucked. But in his home later, I'd sit for hours next to Uncle Sheldon as he played the piano—sat right there next to him on the bench where I saw another use for hands as his moved magically over the black and white keys in a perfect balance of gentleness and strength. Instead of commanding a Sherman tank as my father had, he'd learned to play the piano and taught music at the local college. He had a big grin and would sometimes put his long arm around me while I sat there. He seemed to understand some fear within me that my father didn't, or couldn't perhaps.

Sheldon's baritone voice harmonized beautifully with the tenor one of Charles, the youngest son, himself a high school teacher in the warmer climate of Florida. He'd come back to the Catskills, too, but not to bring home chickens. Charles was single and loved to talk about women, especially if they wore tight skirts. A scarlet birthmark spread across his right cheek from some seeming flame that started on his neck and that he tried to hide by wearing wildly colored tropical shirts

57

and by always having a tan. As a little boy I was scared of

him because of that mark on his face but later came to love

him deeply in his loneliness.

THE BIRTHMARK

No matter what he did—
the Silver Cross for valor,
the powder he'd cover
his right cheek with
like gauze on a wound,
his Florida tan—no matter,
his was a mask he couldn't take off,
rising like flame from the collar
of his tropical shirt
everyone noticed first,

my Uncle Charles
with the map on his face
as he called it,
to not get lost, so he said,
my baby sister giggling,
bouncing on his knee
each Christmas
when he'd come to visit,
his bags full of presents
as he reached to hug me
and I ran away,
afraid to touch it,
the burn from birth
that made Charles different,

though when I did once,

sneaking up
where he slept on our couch,
it felt the same
to my tender hand
as my father's face
after he shaved, my uncle
like my sister in her crib
sound asleep as I traced
the scarlet coast for his house,
my fingers trembling, barely touching,
not wanting to hurt him anymore.

His isolation brought him home every holiday and family

reunion but not out of weakness. During the war, he'd flown

dozens of missions over Germany as a B-29 pilot, and before

that, as a ball-turret gunner in that aircraft's plastic bubble, all

alone in there with nothing below him but air. One tough guy

with one tough burden, my Uncle Charles. I guess my father

knew his little brother was gay and, aware of that secret,

worried about him even more. My old man was full of the age's

normal prejudices but never once did I hear him say an evil

thing about homosexuals. I think now about the current issue

involving gays in the military and those who worry about it.

They should have known my Uncle Charles, a real patriot.

Alfred would sometimes make it to the farm, but he was

even more henpecked than I in the chicken coop. Plus, he was usually broke. "The best wing shot in this county," my father said of him once, but after the war Alfred never went hunting again and sought the serenity of water. He didn't talk much, so what I learned from him was by example when he'd take me to the river. "Trout don't have scales," was all he said once, and then I watched as he dipped his hands in the water before releasing a big fat brook trout. He did so, I discovered later from books about fishing, because dry hands take the protective slime off a trout and make it vulnerable to disease. For his own quiet reasons, Alfred liked keeping things alive and did so long before "catch and release" was ever heard of. I remember how he'd stare into the water for minutes after letting some whopper go as if remembering something, or trying to forget.

Irish as a boiled potato, my mother's brother was shaped like one, too. Ironically, my Uncle Donald was born the same year as my father, but no two men could have been more opposite. Childlike, childish, and childless, Don was my playmate during the summers that my many siblings and I would spend at my grandparents' place in New Hampshire. The world in his eyes

was always in flight, always fantastic. We'd sit on the

lakeshore sometimes for hours, this man in his forties and his

devoted nephew of six, and stare at the sky.

THE LOST BRIGADE

My Uncle Donald always knew the weather.
"Had to, during the war," he told me, "in Alaska,"
as we stood on the steps of our cabin in New Hampshire,
this strange, middle-aged man and I,
scanning the skies for Zeroes—
"I hear 'em. Doncha? Doncha, through the clouds?"—
but I heard nothing, saw only the lake, its surface
the color of pewter before a storm, and my uncle
cupping his troubled brow with his hands
like a soldier with field glasses, his blue eyes blank
and far, far away.

        He'd been a member, I learned years later,
of "The Lost Brigade," the men shipped to the Arctic
in 1942 to guard the Aleutians, those stepping-stones
the ancient Asians crossed centuries ago,
and on Umnak Island Uncle Don gazed west for months
toward Kiska, the island base of the Japanese
fifty miles away.

        Taking turns in twelve-hour shifts,
he and the others of "The Lost Brigade" stared across an open
   tundra
seemingly forever, watching for cracks, some small fracture
in the steel-gray weld of sea and sky, blinded finally

61

by all they did not see. Forgotten on Umnak for nearly two
    years,
Private Donald Heffernan went insane, had to be shipped
back to the States, and by the state,
put away.

       "He saw God's foot on the treadle of the Loom,"
Melville says of Pip, the cabin-boy swept from the Pequod
into the sea, gone mad from that immensity. And my
    uncle?—
a priest without beads, mumbling to himself, an old man now
in his dead parents' house on St. Pete Beach
where he's piled a fort of old papers
deep as snow on any tundra, and boarded up the doors.
From there last week, hurricane season, they dragged him off
screaming about devils in the distance
to a locked ward at the Florida V.A.,
a room without windows.
             Donald's had enough of sky
though he knows the weather, the gathering clouds
a squadron's thunder
so far away.

While my father was making money, my maternal uncle

spent his time inventing, or making plans to at least, because he

never got beyond the planning stage, and the blueprint in his

mind for that single-man helicopter built from my pogo-stick

never took off.

But what fun I had in his dreaming, something my father

must have been jealous of, because *his* dreams were always so practical and so often came true. His business success and Donald's obvious failure to ever make a dime led me, son and nephew, to that great American crossroads: one leading to work; the other, to wonder. I have always thought of Walt Whitman's first initials in these terms: *w*ork and *w*onder. Walt certainly tried to incorporate both, but not so my old man who didn't like it much when I would "loaf and invite my soul," as Whitman says at the beginning of "Song of Myself."

But to his credit—a word I choose with purpose here to speak of his emotional investment—my father understood that Donald had been wounded, too, but not as my father literally had, the shrapnel raking his left leg raw, but deep within, and I never once heard him mock this zany, sad clown of a man.

When my brother and my son and I got together last Christmas, I felt the way my father must have sometimes—I felt left out. You could even say I was a little jealous as I watched them shake hands, then embrace. Brendan, my son, is now in his late teens, a particularly difficult time for a father and son, but he was immediately at ease and laughing with his

Uncle Brian. How, I wondered, standing to the side?—how can they be so quickly at ease? Why is it so difficult for my son and me to be the same way?

When Odysseus goes off to war, he leaves the education of his son in the hands of Mentor, a trusted counselor and guide. Homer thinks so much of this uncle figure that he has the goddess of wisdom, Athena, assume his voice and shape. In his search for his missing father, it is to Mentor that Telemachus turns, but what can "Unc" teach that lonely, confused, and sometimes angry boy?

That he is his father's son and no one else's. Whether they mean to or not, uncles provide a necessary male image from which the son may catch a glimpse of his father the way we catch a surprising one of ourselves in those multi-sided mirrors in the haberdasher's dressing room. Perhaps a new suit might change who we are, but it won't, any more than an uncle can finally ever be the father. Just ask Hamlet.

My uncles were my measure. They helped me to find my father, to learn who he really was. I wonder what my nephew will discover about his own in the odd reflection of me? And

when some brat lays him flat in the school-yard and grinds his

sweet face in the grit, will he cry "uncle" as I did through my

bloodied lips? And while "crying uncle" is today regarded as

an Americanism, history tells us that its origins go all the way

back to the Roman Empire. Roman lads when beset by a bully,

would be forced to say "Patrue, mi Patruissimo," or "Uncle, my

best Uncle," in order to surrender and be freed. Will my

nephew know he's really calling "father," that word for many

sons so difficult to say?

TOAD

The mad uncle
nobody loves but the children.
How they squeal as he dances
hatless
in the rain.

The frog is a prince,
elegant
in his emerald jacket—
the toad, a jester,
his coat of warts, brown motley.

Once, before time,
the toad had a beautiful voice,
sang all evening
in the grass—
sang so sweetly that birds
pecked the music from his throat.

All the songs of birds
are the toad's
hopping at the feet of kids
for laughs,
the old soft-shoe.

THE NEST

Found in the limbs by my son
walking the wind in the apple
the reach and hold of his climbing
the fluttering down of leaves

Held in his palm to the house
a hollow of woven reeds
of hair from the rubbings of deer
skin from the shed of a snake

Set by his bed on the bureau
by the wash of ocean in shells
the husk of a locust still singing
the silent horn of a snail

Heard in his sleep as song
a bird as bright as blood
pecking the breath from blossoms
to feed the beaks of its young

ICE

If the earth
in its waking
remembers rain, grass,
the scent of flowers,

then in its sleep
it dreams of ice,
of wind again
across the glacier

the way we hear
winter nights
when sound
travels for miles:

in the distance,
the scraping of stones;
through the thin air,
a father's voice.

NOBODY'S HOME

"So, you ask me the name I'm known by, Cyclops?
I will tell you. . . .
Nobody--that's my name. Nobody--"
--The Odyssey

"Guernsey—that's an odd name to have," said the
bespectacled teller, squinting at my passport. And so it is back
in the United States where there are not many of us, but it
shouldn't be too strange a name here, I thought—not here on
Guernsey Island. I'd already seen it half-a-dozen times on the
ride in from the airport, branded on service trucks and
buildings, and now again on the very bank where I was
counting my pound notes. Why, even *they* had "Guernsey" on
them because, as I was discovering, this independent little
island near the English Channel has its own currency.

"Odd" or not, at least they spell it right, I said to myself, a
relief from home where "like the cows" is what I've always told
those trying to write my name. *Our* name, I should say,
because I'd come to Guernsey Island to represent my family and
to find out where we'd come from, the search for roots an
American pursuit no matter the color of skin.

69

This trip and its timing were also of special importance to my four siblings and me. A decade ago our father had disappeared from a VA hospital in rural Pennsylvania. His acute Parkinson's Disease led him to wander off, and he did so for good one day in May. My brother, our sisters, and I took part in a massive search to find him but he'd simply vanished, and though that was years ago, I know that deep inside I'm still searching. What better place to do so on the tenth anniversary of his disappearance than the island that bears our father's name?

And what a place it is, too: twenty-six square miles of granite coastline and lush green valleys off the coast of France where roughly sixty-five thousand people live and work or have retired. "The happiest people on earth," according to a survey reported in the New York *Times* a few years back, and as impossible as such a survey might seem, the "Guernseyman" and woman have every right to be so happy: the taxes they pay at the flat rate of twenty percent go directly to the island's own government, the "states" of Guernsey (taxation *with* representation, that is); the weather is always temperate, kept so by the Gulf Stream--it stayed around 65 the week in May I was there; and most people live on locally caught fish and homegrown vegetables while breathing sea-fresh air scented by over sixty varieties of wildflowers that paint the island in yellows, pinks, and blues.

Such travel-poster facts alone would be enough to attract anyone to this paradise, but I'd come for reasons far less defined, ones I hoped to discover. I jokingly sought to find some long-lost and very wealthy uncle—heirless, of course— but found to my confusion not a single Guernsey in the phone book. It occurred to me later that a name is more important when we leave a place than when we're there. It's the little bit of soil we carry with us as Leonardo did "da Vinci," or college students do with a decal of their alma mater on the rear windshield of the family car.

According to an article by Gregory Stevens-Cox supplied to me by the island's archivist, the earliest known Guernsey in the New World probably sailed with Jacques Cartier in 1535 on his second voyage when he discovered the St. Lawrence River. One "Guillaume de Guerneze" is listed on that voyage's manifest. "Guillaume," as the archivist, Dr. Ogier, informed me, was frequently a name associated with bastard children, so maybe that sixteenth century uncle of mine was searching like me for more than just a place to spend a week one spring. Maybe he was looking for his father, too.

Ideally, sailing to the island, instead of flying, would have been my choice, coming back to this imagined home the way others like "Guillaume" had left it centuries ago. I wanted the excitement of seeing its coastline from a distance on the horizon: the island rising and falling in front of me, but *there*, green and rooted. I wanted to be Odysseus, I guess, home after so many years, but stepping from the noisy, two-engine plane onto the island's small runway, I was just me. No mythic hero, just me and my memories.

"That smell," I said to myself, stretching from the cramped plane and breathing in the Guernsey air. "I know that smell," and I was suddenly back in the dairy farms of upstate New

72

York where my father grew up. I was greeted not by the usual fumes of fossil fuels but by the rich and fertile smell of cow manure. While not ambrosia to everyone's nostrils, the smell of something organic, of grass and growth, and at an airport no less, would suggest to anyone that they'd arrived in a different kind of world. For me, it was one much like my father's private Ithaca: Schoharie County in the Catskills where we went each spring to reconnect the family ties and where I learned which end of a cow to milk.

Incredibly, out on that tarmac, I had quickly traveled back to my father's world before he'd moved downstate to the hurried pace of turnpikes and his life of sales. I stood there elated, then suddenly depressed: the closest my father ever came to this special place were the beaches of Normandy, thirty miles away, around June 6, 1944. I was born that year, although my father never saw his first son for many months after. He went to shore in the second wave of troops, and the many German gun emplacements on this peaceful island suggest how terrifying that must have been.

The next morning, with a camera, not a gun, in hand, I set out on my first full day on Guernsey to make a Christmas scrapbook for my siblings and my kids, and for their many new cousins. Snapping close-ups of purple foxglove and panoramas of endless white daisies, I found myself stepping down into a ditch--for irrigation, I figured, but it was far deeper than that, chest-high. Entangled in vines, I fought my way along the rock-edged trench until in front of me there was a hollow, a hidden opening in concrete, and I climbed in.

Whew! Talk about smells! The stench of a thousand "pissoirs" practically blinded me. Gone was the bouquet of the endless flowers outside. Gone, too, that rich fertile fullness I smelled at the airport. Now I was indeed Odysseus, but in the Cyclops' cave where the one-eyed giant hadn't stopped peeing since classical Greece, so it seemed. Or more accurately, six decades ago when the Nazi gunners who once stood in this same battery could have blown away a man just like my father had he come ashore fifty yards below.

Remnants of war like that emplacement are everywhere on

Guernsey. They are as hidden, too, just as they were in my father's imagination. In the five years the island was occupied, using captured Belgians and Poles as labor, the Nazis constructed an underground hospital and tunneled through the island's Precambrian granite to make dormitories and fuel depots. Some of these locations remained a secret until well after the war. One such tunnel goes under St. Saviour, a small and lovely church nestled in a wooded valley. Cynically, the Germans figured no one would bomb a church and so such tunnels would be safe. They also posted sentincls in St. Saviour's picturesque steeple for the same reason.

Keeping his war-time memories in his own kind of underground, my father never talked about the war other than to say it was over, but I believe his experiences in it drove him to work as hard as he did. Both running to and running from, he set out on his own to sell life insurance and was a financial success. He'd been hollowed out inside, however, and those trips back to the farmland were meant to make him whole. The war had displaced my father just as it did the people of his namesake island and, as it did, of course, around the world. When the Germans took Guernsey—they could do so because of the island's proximity to France, and they wanted to as a symbol of taking something British—many of the women and children were evacuated to Great Britain and the deep fabric of this island was forever torn.

In a country pub one day for lunch, I couldn't help but notice the accent of a gentleman near me who didn't sound the least bit "Guernsey," a distinct, non-English dialect that's tinged with remnants of Norman patois. He sounded more Scots, like Sean Connery. Discovering more in pubs than I did in books, I learned of his separation from his homeland at three years old and of his formative years spent in northern England. "It was tough to come back," he said, "and my brother didn't." Just as our Civil War displaced New Englanders and Southerners alike, so too did the young of this island go to the mainland because of war, dividing families, making new voices.

Or making you question your old way of speaking, as happened to my father. Despite the many self-improvement courses he'd rise before dawn to study, "haywire," "hogwash," and "happy as a heifer in heat" remained his favorite expressions. In the suburbs of northern New Jersey, a long cultural way from where he grew up, such language didn't help him get into the fancy golf clubs to make important financial connections. He never went to college yet wanted people to think he had.

His words, however, were not the educated ones from Princeton or Yale but from the farm, his metaphors from some place like Guernsey Island. In suburbia such poetry gets you nowhere, and so he struggled even harder to succeed. Like the mythic Willy Loman, my father was best a carpenter and planter; like the missing Doug Guernsey, Willy would have been happy here, too.

They would have loved the hundreds of greenhouses where for generations the island has produced most of the tomatoes, especially the cherry, for the United Kingdom. Those little broiled rubies that accompany the Royalty's bacon and egg each morning probably came from under these buildings of glass.

77

Though fragile, they are powerful symbols when set against the Nazis' cold bunkers which, like the Cyclops' monomaniacal gaze, are blank and pitiless, waiting to feast on human flesh. In number and spirit, however, the greenhouses win: they are everywhere, gathering light. So many times, when looking across a valley, I could see a sheen like water: each long glass house, the pool of a river.

And, yes, there are cows, colored golden russet with patches of cream, ruminating on it all. I remember as a kid trying to milk one, but I went on to do other things better: a child, like many Americans in the year 2000, of the suburbs and college. But I was back now on one of those week-long trips to our family farm. On a green, green island, "Nobody's" first son had landed. I'd hiked this little world of war and peace without a map in a symbolic search for my father and found what I didn't know I was looking for: me.

The last night on Guernsey I walked a few blocks from my hotel down to a point along the beach. I climbed up on some rocks that looked curiously organized, a large flat piece of

granite horizontal to some huge verticals that balanced it. From
there I could look east toward Normandy better than from any
of the German bunkers near it, and there were several. Little
did I know until I uncovered a vine-tangled sign that I was
perched upon a Druid dolmen. Having, alas, no flask to lift a
toast to eternity, I took a piece of gum from my pocket instead
and sat there chewing like my bovine cousins. "Like the island,"
I'll say from now on, knowing truly how to spell my name.

EISENSTAEDT'S KISS

I dream for my parents it was just like this:
the anonymous sailor, the anonymous nurse,

her head in his arm, his hand at her waist,
on Times-Square that day in August

about when my father came down the ramp
and they kissed like those strangers I hope,

bending together, my mother and father,
curve into curve, these mythical lovers.

MAPS

Those who've been to war love maps.
They keep them everywhere: in pockets, drawers,
the glove box of cars and stacked by the toilet.
Maps are what they read, these poems for soldiers
who hear in the lines the whir of blades,
who smell in the colors the char of smoke.

They know the hidden meaning of rivers,
the true symbol of water, how dry a last breath—
that here, spread flat on the kitchen table,
are really mountains, the strategic home of gods.
For those such as these, myth is truth,
and this paper you touch, a metaphor for earth.

DISTANCE

There is a house across the field.

From the other side where I started
it did not seem so far away.

I have been walking towards it a long time,
through mud, the turned ground,
and now this snow beginning to fall.

The house has grown
only slightly larger
and I think I see someone outside.

Yes, I am sure of it—
people, two or three, beside the house,
moving about.

I am waving, suddenly waving,
but out so far in this openness of field
will not be seen or heard.

Faster, walk faster,
before they go inside
whoever they are, before they close the door
across the field
where nothing is growing,
the gray, flat horizon.

DIGGING TO AMERICA

When I was a little kid, I was sure I could dig to China. If you dug a hole deep enough, the grown-ups said, that's where you'd come out. The big tall plumber said it was so when he came to see why our pipes were leaking. He said they were that deep, and my father, who told him he could fix them himself for less, seemed to agree. He did until he hit something that got him all wet. Then he started yelling more about the hot place and where the plumber should go other than China.

Oddly, the Orient and hell seemed to be in the same location, underground, as were so many other things back in the Eisenhower years, like the bomb shelters we had to practice walking calmly down into, following the big yellow and black signs to the safety of a church basement or school gym. Or the truth about sex, kept hidden from us like buried treasure, and the secret intimacies of family and neighborhood life cloaked in Republican propriety until Elvis and *Peyton Place* came along.

My good friend, Freddy Gumm, who lived next door and was already ten, shared my fascination for whatever was under. I guess that's why he liked looking up girls' dresses so much. The two of us had been digging like crazed puppies in the bushes behind his house for a couple of weeks. We were nearly in Shanghai when my father, on his way home from Mr. Pumphrey's, dropped suddenly out of sight.

He'd gone over for a night-cap, one of those that lasts till sun-up, and was taking the short-cut home. The plywood board we'd covered with leaves wasn't strong enough to hold his wobbly foot and down he went to China, a four-foot drop that got him muddy and mad as hell, the word I wasn't supposed to hear that he used again. It served him right, my mother said, who was prudish about booze and probably wondered where he really went. I was about to have a sister again, or maybe with luck my first brother, and she said some things to my father that made him even madder at me. An eight-year-old in those times knew only rumors about where

babies came from, and God and Communism and all that was
mysterious about life were mixed together in my imagination.

Fred's old man and mine stood watch over us like prison
guards until we'd filled our tunnel up. China could not have
been far, the hole seemed that deep. I can still hear our
shovels scraping, the rocks and clods falling back into place, a
sound that soon would make a mockery of all our fanciful
digging. Freddy's little brother was only five or six months
old when he didn't wake up from his nap a few weeks later.
"SIDS" is what we'd call it now, but there wasn't a name for it
then. No matter: he simply died without reason one April day,
snug in his carriage near the bushes where we dug. The sun
was even shining.

Freddy Gumm was the toughest kid on the block and could
throw a baseball higher than anyone, so when I saw him
crying for the first time, I knew it was okay to do so too,
especially when he moved away the next year after his
parents, who always had the best candy at Halloween and
seemed so nice, got divorced. The hole we dug together has

taken on huge meaning ever since. Finally getting to China a few months back, I realized that had I been a Chinese kid, I'd perhaps have been digging to America instead. I wondered where I would have surfaced. Little did I know that I'd come crawling out in my old neighborhood like my luckless father in the Gumm's back yard—that I'd end up just where I'd started, at home.

My son and I were on a train to Hangzhou, the city Marco Polo called the loveliest in the world. Marco had taken an overland route instead of under, and Brendan and I had come by sea, its watery cradle reenacted by the rails whose rocking had put my son to sleep. He'd been up too late, hanging out with other Semester at Sea students on our ship and had slipped into dreamland with his head on my shoulder. I was a faculty member for the fall voyage, and my son was able to come along to finish his last term in college. Now in his early twenties, he would not have rested his head that way as he had once, but we were crowded in by the many Chinese, so there he was leaning against me, a little kid again but snoring like a man, his Red Sox cap tilted askew.

When he was the age of Freddy Gumm's baby brother, how could I have imagined such a scene?—dozens of curious Chinese staring at my son and me on a train through the mist and drizzle of rice fields. What were they thinking, I wondered, feeling a bit uneasy from their intense looks, their constant watching. I was programmed in the '50's to believe that under those straw hats lurked the lust of Communism, a mystery that rivaled even sex in legend and power. I'd hid underground from these people, or from the Russians, at least. They were all Communists, so what did it matter as the sirens sounded every Tuesday at school. And why wouldn't I hide! After all, the Commie Chinks reproduce faster than we do, I heard in a barber shop one day. Seven months and they hatch, one guy said; more like six, the big man with the crew-cut replied.

In fourth grade and good at math at the time, I quickly figured how many more Chinese there would be than

Americans and here they were all before me, leering and scary, until my son's cap fell off and skidded across the train floor and everyone was suddenly laughing. It came to rest at the feet of a tiny woman, huddled alone and very old, who picked it up as if it were holy, staring at the crimson "B." For some reason, as she stood and bowed before my groggy son, a powerful deja-vu experience washed over me. Where had this happened before?—the way she held the hat in front of her and returned to him his emblem of home, more lines in her face than I'd ever seen in anyone. I felt at ease on the train and in China from then on but was unnerved by my own vague memories.

In Vietnam a few weeks later, I watched that same cap disappear into the Cu Chi Tunnels, a network of underground passages originally part of the Viet Minh's fight against the French but repaired and rebuilt by the Viet Cong. Like Freddy and me they dug all of the 200-kilometer system by hand. Their trap doors, however, were far more effective than ours, invisible to the enemy eye or dog-sniffing nose. In their own

88

way, and a brutal one it was, the Viet Cong were digging to America, using the tunnels for mounting surprise attacks against our troops.

Seeing my son descend into one ahead of me, then turn back to give me the peace sign, a grin on his face, made me shudder, as if he were the point-man on a patrol. From the dark room of my memory came a picture of my father taken during the Second World War. Climbing into a tank, helmet on and waving, he was smiling like Brendan. I vividly remember how I used to stare at that hole in the top of the tank where his body disappeared.

I have no idea what I was trying to see. The wheels and gears, I guess, whatever was down there, as mysterious to a boy as the facts of life, and death. My mother always claimed my father was never the same after the war, that he never smiled quite the same boyish way again as he did in the photo from Fort Sill before he went into combat. Whatever was inside that tank took something inside of him away.

I was my son's age now when President Johnson sent the first big wave of troops to Vietnam, and like many young men and women at the time, I wanted to believe that what my country was doing was right. We were as naive as my son at Cu Chi and my father in boot camp, until the horrors of Vietnam came home to us on the screen or in a plastic bag. "And babies?" Mike Wallace asked. "And babies," the anonymous soldier replied, America's collective heart stopping during that television newscast, the truth of the Mi Lai massacre revealed to us all. America could kill babies on purpose?! I cried again, just as I did with Freddy, and so did the country, a hideous secret unearthed.

Memory is a labyrinth of tunnels that are somehow all connected like Cu Chi. My father had told me to clean out the leaves from the hedges, the spring chore I hated most, and I was deep into the briars when I heard a noise I'd never heard before and never heard again until those scenes from Mi Lai. A moaning sound, too low to be a cry, but a crying that went with it. There are no words for this kind of grief, and I stood up to see where such a sound was coming from.

On the sun-porch next door I could see Freddy's mom rocking forwards and back like someone sick and about to throw up, but there was something in her hands, something that she held out in front of her the way Father Davis carried God in the chalice at church. And on the television screen there she was again, running from the flames, the torched thatch behind her, clutching her soft bundle of pain. And was that her, too, on our trip to Hangzhou, retrieving my son's innocence, his cap with its mysterious red symbol that she cradled like an offering? Is this where I'd seen that old, old woman before, next door?

When my country dug to China in the early sixties, by intention or mistake, it got to Vietnam instead. When I found myself digging to America while in China and Vietnam, I ended up in my old back yard. I had heard there for the first time in my life the deepest sound there is: the sound of sorrow at the death of a child. Never before had I felt so alone, and I was afraid as if I'd traveled to some place far away where not only the language was strange but even the very sounds. Like China, perhaps, or Vietnam.

That's where I was that April day, though I hadn't gone anywhere; that's where I had returned forty-five years later, despite being on the other side of the world. Digging to America meant unearthing my deepest memories, and I was beginning to see how deep were the underground connections between me and my nation's recent history. "And babies?" "Yes, and babies." The train to Hangzhou, the tunnels of Cu Chi, had brought me back to that hole in Freddy Gumm's yard and the sound of the earth falling back into place.

Where we grew up and the experiences we had in that time which is also a place are the soil on our boots wherever we go. After Freddy and I had finished our secret digging for the day, I hid my shoes in the basement so I wouldn't track mud on the carpet the way my grumbling father did. But there is no washing off the earth when we dig in it deeply. It sticks to the spirit and is our history.

FORTUNATE SONS

My Uncle Sheldon never went to war,
the oldest son exempt by law
to carry on our family name,
to care for the farm.
From milking cows his hands grew strong
those cold, Catskill mornings,
and gentle, too, bathed in milk,
his fingers long against the firm,
pink udders, and by the time his brothers
came back from overseas,
he'd taught himself to play the piano.

His brothers—
Alfred, Douglas, Charles—
he calmed with those hands
when they'd wake in their beds like boys
to the high whine of shells
and brute fact of lead,
the rhythm, like milking, of his fingers at the keys
stilling the rattling windows
with music like steam, grassy and sweet
from the buckets rising, filling with sleep
the house they each were born in.

BACK ROAD

Winter mornings
driving past
I'd see these kids
huddled like grouse
in the plowed ruts
in front of their shack
waiting for the bus,
three small children
bunched against the drifts
rising behind them.

This morning
I slowed to wave
and the smallest,
a stick of a kid
draped in a coat,
grinned and raised
his red, raw hand,
the snowball
packed with rock
aimed at my face.

THE SCOUT

Just another beggar kid
in the cinders and soot
outside Belgrade, working the train I took
through Yugoslavia to Greece
the winter we were shelling Iraq—

like so many I'd seen each stop, these strays
walking the tracks, window to window,
palms up, filthy as the roadside snow,
no more than nine or ten years old,
scavenging for cigarettes.

But this one, this kid, this kid and his cap,
a Davy Crockett coonskin cap
complete with ringed tail, amazing!—this boy
with his frontier hat, on his own
in the crush of crowd, the blowing paper.

Leaning out the double glass I see the widows
heavy on their canes, a few old men
in dark suits and everywhere soldiers,
groups of them all over, smoking, pacing,
rechecking their orders—and there,

darting in between them all,
the bad boy, the bandit, that young pioneer—
the soldiers like older brothers
he scoots around as they grab, laughing,
for his pelt of hair, but in the lurch

and screech of steel, the hiss of steam
as we start south to the sea, he slips their grasp
and coon-tail waving, escapes

behind the black and red graffiti sprayed
like war paint on the station's wall,

out of the wind, lighting up.

AT THE GRAVE OF THOMAS LINCOLN

Not far from where I live in east central Illinois, the father
of Abraham Lincoln lies buried. Though I've lived out here in
this open land for over two decades, I had not visited Thomas
Lincoln's grave until last spring, two years after my own father
disappeared. Pop suffered from acute Parkinson's Disease but
was able, on occasion, to dress himself and shuffle about. He
did so that fateful May morning and wandered away from the
VA hospital into the forests of rural Pennsylvania. Frail and
confused, he surely had died, but despite an exhaustive search,
we never found where.

In an effort to deal with my grief and confusion, I had taken
up long distance running and on one of my ten-mile jaunts,
found myself trotting by Shiloh Cemetery, the resting place of
Thomas Lincoln. I, too, needed a rest and sought one there
where Abraham Lincoln once stood, looking down at the stone
with his father's name chiseled into it. I wanted such a marker
for my own father; I wanted him to be at peace so that our

family could be as well. I guess you could say I was a little jealous of that special son and began to imagine his voice as he lowered his head and whispered to his father.

What he said, and especially how he said it, became an obsession of mine after that visit. The President-elect had come there the last time on January 31, 1861. He was off to Washington the next day to be inaugurated. I felt like an eavesdropper, my ear at the wall of time as I tried to hear this incredible moment of a son speaking to father about what lay before him. Did he ask for advice? Did he say thank you? Did the past come back with all its difficulties, and did they argue? I wanted to know because I, too, was now a fatherless son.

I attempted to deal with this connection I felt by writing a poem, but struggled with point of view. Finally, I realized that I had to write this in Lincoln's voice, not my own or my father's or Thomas Lincoln's or some third-person's--a dramatic monologue, that is, set on that very day in January, the air raw in this openness, and windy as only the prairie can be. The monologue's time and place were the easy part, but what did

Lincoln sound like? I had to know and turned to his letters and speeches to find out.

I began thumbing through the first of the Library of America's two-volume set of Lincoln's work, the 1832-1858 writings edited by Don E. Fehrenbacher. Among a group of 1846 political letters was a strikingly familiar sight: words in a vertical shape that didn't go all the way to the right-hand margin—words that looked a lot like poetry. Abraham Lincoln wrote poetry!? Amazing! I knew he split rails and learned to read by candlelight, but I'd never heard about the poems. Besides, an ambitious young lawyer-politician is hardly someone we think of as penning verse. What might have been so important for him to take the time to do so, I wondered? Could it be that something "hurt" him into poetry, as has been said of poets before, but not of future presidents?

"My Childhood-Home I See Again," the poem I found there, was actually written in two separate parts that were included in letters to Andrew Johnston, a former colleague of Lincoln's in the Illinois House and a budding poet himself. In another letter,

Lincoln sent along a third poem called, "The Bear Hunt," and humbly refers to all of his poetry as "doggerel." "I am not at all displeased with your proposal to publish the poetry," Lincoln says to Johnston, however. He does want his name "suppressed," so he says, for "I have not sufficient hope of the verses attracting any favorable notice to tempt me to risk being ridiculed for having written them." The two halves of "Childhood-Home" did finally appear in the Quincy, Illinois Whig and with Lincoln's name, so perhaps this legendary man was just like any other beginning poet: at once shy, nervous, and proud about what he had written.

Honest Abe was also being honest—the work is stylized and sentimental—and the distinctive voice I was searching for was not in these little-known poems, alas. It is, of course, in the prose, but I'm convinced that Lincoln's practice with lines and, as I learned later, his constant reading and reciting of poetry helped make him the speech writer he was. Of equal importance, the content of these poems hints at a vision in the making, revealing this dark-browed man's nostalgic personality as he ranges from troubling thoughts of home to a rollicking ride through the country, hunting bears.

Writing to Johnston on April 18, 1846, Lincoln acknowledges a parody of "The Raven" that his friend had sent along but admits that he has never read Poe's original. He also discusses another poem that he'd read some years before "in a straggling form in a newspaper," one he would "give all I am worth . . . to be able to write"--a poem that scholars are sure was William Knox's "Mortality," a very somber piece. He concludes this letter with some stanzas of his own that he "was led to write under the following circumstances." To summarize, Lincoln had gone back to Indiana helping to campaign in 1844 and while there, had visited the site "where [his] mother and only sister were buried." The result of that visit is the first part of what became "My Childhood-Home."

Despite its predictable meter from Protestant hymns ("common meter") and all kinds of graveyard-school poeticisms, the poem is still oddly touching. Or at least I found it to be, no doubt because of what had recently happened in my family's life, but also because of what I knew of Lincoln's own sorrows and of his later heroic struggle to keep the national "home" together, never having had a permanent one of his own. These stanzas are typical of Lincoln's somber tone:

As dusky mountains please the eye
  When twilight chases day;
As bugle-notes that, passing by,
  In distance die away;

As leaving some grand waterfall,
  We, lingering, list its roar--
So memory will hallow all
  We've known, but know no more.

          ***

The friends I left that parting day,
  How changed, as time has sped!
Young childhood grown, strong manhood gray,
  And half of all are dead.

I hear the loved survivors tell
  How nought from death could save,
Till every sound appears a knell,
  And every spot a grave.

One of those friends he left, one of those "loved survivors," is the subject of the next section which he sent Johnston half a year later. Based on the same visit to Indiana, these lines deal

with "an insane man" from his hometown whom Lincoln

identifies as Matthew Gentry. Matthew once went to school

with Abe, but at nineteen became "unaccountably" mad. The

poet Lincoln found him in this same "wretched condition" in

1844, and in a "poetizing mood," wrote thirteen quatrains about

the man's plight. In form and content these are a focused

extension of the previous stanzas and underwent only minor

changes when Lincoln joined them all together:

But here's an object more of dread
  Than ought the grave contains--
A human form with reason fled,
  While wretched life remains.

Poor Matthew! Once of genius bright,
  A fortune-favored child--
Now locked for aye, in mental night,
  A haggard mad-man wild.

***

How then you strove and shrieked aloud,
  Your bones and sinews bared;
And fiendish on the gazing crowd,
  With burning eye-balls glared--

And begged, and swore, and wept and prayed
  With maniac laugh joined--

103

How fearful were those signs displayed
  By pangs that killed thy mind!

"The Bear Hunt," sent to Johnston in February, 1847, is a

major change of pace and would have confirmed what many in

Washington thought of this lanky mid-westerner, that he was a

hick at heart. Full of energy and nineteenth-century country fun,

the poem showed me another side of Lincoln, who apparently

was able to have a hearty laugh at what "pompous, two-legged

dogs there be," as well as feel for the plight of his fellow man as

he does for Matthew Gentry. Despite its continual end-stopped

lines, "The Bear Hunt" races along on monosyllabic paws and

hooves in pursuit of both its burly quarry and Lincoln's

concluding moral about man's false pride. These parts of the

"chace" pick up the pace:

On press his foes, and reach the ground,
  Where's left his half munched meal;
The dogs, in circles, scent around,
  And find his fresh made trail.

With instant cry, away they dash,
  And men as fast pursue;
O'er logs they leap, through water splash,
  And shout the brisk halloo.
                    * * *

And round, and round the chace now goes,
  The world's alive with fun;
Nick Carter's horse, his rider throws,
  And more, Hill drops his gun.

Now sorely pressed, bear glances back,
  And lolls his tired tongue;
When as, to force him from his track,
  An ambush on him sprung.

Given the earthiness of Lincoln's subject here, I was not surprised when I learned later that his two favorite poets were Shakespeare and Burns, lads of the fields themselves. Lincoln is reported to have walked the hallways of the White House late at night reciting lines from *Macbeth*, the tragedy he liked most. Political themes appealed to him most for obvious reasons, but he also loved the figure of Falstaff. He had his critical opinions, too. Writing to the actor James H. Hackett in 1863, he said, "Unlike you gentlemen of the profession, I think the soliloquy in *Hamlet* commencing `O, my offence is rank' surpasses that commencing `To be, or not to be.'"

So, Lincoln was more like Claudius than Hamlet when visiting his father's grave, I thought after reading this. "A man to double business bound," unable to pray sincerely like that ambitious brother caught between love and hate. "Bow, stubborn knees," Lincoln may well have said that January morning, trying to find the right words to say good-by to his father with whom he had had a difficult relationship. He had to find those right words, too, on November 19, 1863, at another, more famous grave site.

And that he certainly did, all 272 of them in the legendary address which is a poem in prose, as Gary Wills makes so clear in his wonderful book, *Lincoln at Gettysburg*. Part inspiration, part perspiration, the writing of the speech is as surrounded by mystery as Coleridge's composition of "Kubla Khan." Myth has it that Lincoln wrote it on the train, hastily on an envelope, his muse the rhythm of the rails. More likely, he worked on it for days, carefully selecting, carefully omitting, for the speech gets a good deal of its richness from what's left out.

For example, "The omission of most coupling words," as Wills states, of what rhetoricians call asyndeton—"We are engaged/ . . . We are met/ . . . We have come/. . ."—an absence of "and's" and "but's," that is, and no transitional adverbs to make them sound like sentences. Instead, these sentences sound like lines, which is why I separated them as if I were quoting a poem. "We can not dedicate/ . . .we can not consecrate/ . . .we can not hallow."

This "telegraphic eloquence," Wills' oxymoron for Lincoln's verse-like precision at Gettysburg, was certainly part of the contemporary technology, one that Lincoln welcomed for practical purposes to keep up with his generals but one that he also made into an art form, epigrammatic, lapidary. He apparently grew very impatient with imprecise language from the War Department which fumbled with messages, and thus the truth, in a way that we have grown used to today. In contrast, here are some of Lincoln's telegrams that Wills gives us that reveal Lincoln's ear for brevity, Shakespeare's "soul of wit":

"Have none of it. Stand firm."

"On that point hold firm, as with a chain of steel."

"Watch it every day, and hour, and force it."

Hard-hitting monosyllables, these crafted miniatures mostly are, but when I listened more closely, I could hear a rise and fall in those one-syllable words: an iambic rhythm, that is, which persuades the recipient of the message more gently. In the first example, Lincoln starts out with a brisk, two-step stride to the door and ends with two hard knocks. The second message is the opposite in form: several stressed syllables followed by a simile in three alternating accented syllables--the same iambic trimeter found in the even lines of a common meter stanza. As in a line of poetry, the comma placement in the third little gem helps create a voice by isolating a moment of time that is more exact than "day" and makes the recipient's two-fisted duty even more urgent.

Lincoln clearly had a sense of words as sounds. He loved theater, he loved mimicry, he loved poetry. From all reports he had a high-pitched tenor voice, not the brawny baritone we might expect and which has been portrayed. More reed in the prairie wind than rumbling roll of the sea. Wills believes that Lincoln was well heard at Gettysburg because of the tone of his voice, but how exactly he emphasized the syllables is anyone's guess. Here's mine.

Lincoln starts with a rhyme, and it would be hard not to put equal emphasis on both "Four" and "score." He begins with a spondee, that is, with two hard stresses like that knock at the door--or more appropriately here, the bang of a drum. The next line is simple iambic: "and seven years ago," followed by the strongly alliterative, "our fathers brought forth upon this continent." But here we have a slight discrepancy between the spoken text and the official written one. In the former, Lincoln included the syllable, "up-" (to "-on") that he omits in print, this slack syllable smoothing the rhythm into iambic and perhaps adding, ever-so-slightly, to the eloquence of hearing. The additionally alliterative, "a new nation," is followed again by iambics that might be broken into lines this way: "conceived in Liberty,/and dedicated to/the proposition that." The spondee Lincoln opened with then returns with "all men," and the first paragraph/stanza concludes with strong assonance, "are created equal."

My little exercise here isn't meant to suggest that Lincoln continually measured his way through words, but that by the time he went to Gettysburg, language had a more natural motion for him, not the studied and stilted formality of his poems more than a decade before. As Wills says, "Lincoln, like most writers of great prose, began by writing bad poetry." An apprenticeship in form and in selecting the right word to fit, which was a lifelong struggle for the studied Lincoln, comes in part from these poetic attempts. This kind of discipline, together with his habit of reciting poetry--of putting voice to words, that is--help make his prose so memorable. Like an Elizabethan actor, he learned to hear in lines, and came to write that way.

What he found the need to write about in a poem like "My Childhood-Home" is also the very stuff of his greatest eloquence in the speeches and letters. What "hurt" him into this poem was visiting the graves of his mother and sister; that is, his sorrow at the early separation from their warmth and companionship. Returning after fifteen years to what he knew of home, as he wrote to Johnston, "aroused feelings in me which were certainly poetry." And hadn't I stopped at Thomas Lincoln's grave because of the same feelings, because of an ache in my heart?

The heartbeat is everywhere in Lincoln's best writing as he attempts to resolve loss with the comforting pulse of the iambic rhythm. For example, in his famous letter to Mrs. Bixby, who had lost five of her sons in battle, the President returns again and again to this consoling rise and fall: "I feel how weak and fruitless must/ be any word of mine . . . I pray that our Heavenly Father may assuage/ . . . the cherished memory of the loved and lost/ . . . the solemn pride that must be yours." (Line breaks mine).

Motherless, he sought the bosom of his stepmother, Sarah Bush Lincoln, and becomes almost mother-like himself in his tender concern for someone like Matthew Gentry, who was neglected by both fate and family. The cradle rocks endlessly and subtly at those most emotional and memorable moments of Lincoln's prose. I hear its rhythm in these concluding words-as-lines from the Second Inaugural Address: "to care for him who shall have borne the battle,/ and for his widow, and his orphan--/to do all which may achieve and cherish/ a just and lasting peace, among ourselves,/ and with all nations." The sophisticated rhymes ("borne," "orphan," "nations") and reassuring rhythms ("lines" one and four, near perfect blank verse) are here in service of the richest of themes.

They are that way, too, at the end of the Gettysburg Address where Lincoln brings down an imagined curtain with a powerful and symbolic rhyme the way Shakespeare closes a scene. And he does so as naturally, the formal training in verse blending memorably with the human voice. Here's how I shaped the final clauses of his famous last sentence into poetry:

" . . .that the nation shall, under God,
   have a new birth of freedom,
   and that this government
   of the people, by the people, for the people,
   shall not perish from the earth."

No doubt there was long applause after he finished, but I'll bet there was also that moment of silence that follows the hearing of a deeply felt poem. We hold our breath and maybe even bow our heads, look down at the earth. Did he call him

Thomas or Father, this man whose family name he'd carried

from birth? With all those stones at Gettysburg, for "those who

struggled here," how could he not think of that one at Shiloh, as

I envision my own father's now. Hat off, the wind harsh out of

the west, the son of Thomas Lincoln had come with "a great

task" before him. He'd come to remember and give thanks,

reasons enough for any poem.

NAMING THE TREES

At the national cemetery in Gettysburg
all the trees have names,
both the family and genus
on small brass plaques at the base of each
to let the visitor know
the kind of oak,
whether red, white or black,
and is this rock or silver maple
looking once like any other
burlapped ball of roots
when it was lowered to earth
those decades after the war.

Colorful names like Tulip Poplar,
Weeping Beech, Buckeye,
Sweet Gum and Ginko—
sounding like nicknames almost, these trees
from every region and state
with broad leaves or skinny,
shiny, dull, or no leaves at all
like the Eastern Hemlock,
but all, all with names every one,
no matter the size and shape
amidst the many anonymous
mute stones in their shade.

IMAGES OF WAR

Looking out the front window of my house
this spring morning, the soft rain greening
the new grass of late March
as civil wars rage daily on the TV screen,

I think of the greenhouses built from glass
once etched with the images of war:
barefoot men in muddy trenches dug
to hold back Grant at Petersburg,

the smoky negatives of their swollen bodies
sold by photographers gone broke
at the end of the war, glass plates
pieced together like cathedral windows

to heat the flats of roses underneath,
to green the new shoots, sunlight
thin at first, eclipsed by the dark of shoeless feet,
by the winter haze of empty hands

shading for a time the plants beneath,
then slowly like mist, like a rain cloud lifting,
slowly vanishing—an eye, the nose, his face—
the glass pure sky, a summer's day.

THE WALL

Someone has opened a giant map
and with the tips of our fingers,
each of us suddenly blind,
we track the black cold of this monument
for names we know
like finding a route home.

Lost here
this damp spring morning,
the cherries exploding like the fourth of July,
we wonder how many maps of Viet Nam
sold those years,
so many strange sounding places.

One of us holds a magnifying glass
to McCarroll, McMorris, McNabb,
small print in the polished stone,
the way a neighbor, say, in Neoga, Illinois,
might have done, late at night
searching that faraway land on his kitchen table,

hearing again the morning paper
thump against the front door,
that boy on his bike in the dark
grown and gone—*what was his name,
that kid from down the block?*—
Khe Sanh, Da Nang, Hanoi.

THE LITTLE STORE

It was a learning lesson for baseball and the country. If we all look back, we can see that baseball helped make this a better country for us all. --Larry Doby

Watching the 1999 All-Star game at Fenway Park was a wonder for any fan. The place itself echoes with history, and because this annual contest was the century's last, all the famed old-timers were there, introduced chronologically to the Beantown faithful and to the nostalgic millions at home like me. But something happened as I was waving my pennant and standing to cheer, something that made me put down my peanuts and Cracker Jacks, something I suddenly remembered: a place in my own baseball past. All those white guys from the early fifties—The Scooter and Yogi, Bobby Feller and Robin Roberts—there they were, shoulder-to-shoulder, tipping their caps. Then out came Larry Doby, trotting from the dugout, the first man of his race to play in the American League. It was then the camera flashed to number 42 on the outfield wall, and there I was again, grass-stained and sweaty, having a Coke at "The Little Store," the soda and ice cream place where we'd go after playing ball. Number 42, retired now by the major leagues, never to be worn again, the late Jackie Robinson's number…

I grew up on a lower middle-class block in the northeast around 1950. Each family had four or five kids. We had six, my old man determined to outdo the guy next door in everything. "Rabbit-row," as my parents named it, was what you might call "pre-subdivision"—that is, there were still lots of old trees on the street, and the small, tidy yards were divided by a head-high tangle of briar-patch shrubs where your ball would always get lost when playing catch. Communism was the national menace and crab grass its secret agent that fathers went back to war against on Saturday mornings.

Determination to succeed ruled the roost—or the "hutch," as my folks might have put it—because our street was fathered by veterans who'd fought the fascists and mothered by women who'd spent their late teens and early twenties, not in college, but supporting the war effort. Hard work and a sense of purpose were the legacy passed on to my generation. Tolerance, sadly, was not—tolerance for beer and whistling at women perhaps, but not for anyone of another color. The neighborhood was all white, but five blocks away was the Negro part of town. Between us and them, however, was the best ball field around, and next to it, on a corner all by itself, stood "The Little Store," a kind of funky, wooden-floored version of a 7-Eleven that to us was almost holy: our reward for running the gauntlet, for risking whatever it was we feared from being in that part of town.

Going to Southwest Park was a little like taking a lead off first when my friend Freddy was pitching. A crafty southpaw already at ten, he had a great pickoff move, and the excitement of being off base with him on the mound was simply too tempting. It was a dare, a test of manhood, the way playing at Southwest was. But the command from home stayed with us like the yell of an invisible coach: "Stay close!" Don't go to that park unless you have someone bigger along, but parents never had the time to take us and an older brother seemed always washing the family car because he'd be getting his license next year. So off we'd sneak alone, risking the wrath of our parents and the imagined danger of our destination, all for the thrill of the game and for our clubhouse celebration at "The Little Store."

This was not yet the time of organized ball for kids my age. Little League may have existed somewhere, but baseball for us was pickup games of two or three on a side, or most of the times, hitting flies to one another. Lugging a couple of Louisville sluggers with Williams or DiMaggio on their labels, plus a ball the color of an old potato from having been tied all winter in a mitt oiled dark brown to make a pocket, we'd cut through the dozens of back yards to the edge of the park. It was there we stopped, however, and it was there we hid in the small patch of woods that stood between two worlds of separate colors.

"I see a few of them over there," Al might say, all of us bunched behind a giant trunk, and we'd wait then for the black kids to leave, or if they didn't, go back home. "Do you think they know they're colored?" Mike asked once as we watched, which was something none of us had ever thought about, I guess, having never thought about being white, until Mike's question that day. Why *would* we, as insulated as we were in our neighborhood, and as reassured as we were each spring by our favorite game whose players, our heroes, could have moved right in next door, all but two of them anyway. For us, there was no reason to think of white as even a color, but we began to as we waited there behind those trees, afraid.

Of what, I'm not exactly sure. Certainly our vague fears had something to do with race, with ugly things we'd heard on the block. Plus, we were a long way from home, so it seemed, and were now at the border of a foreign land, and after a harrowing journey besides. Not only were we disobeying our parents but we had ventured through a mapless forest in doing so, dark and forbidding as those still-wooded house lots were to us, the ones unsold because overpriced, to keep a certain people out, no doubt. But who knew that at nine years old.

The very size of the park was troubling, too. Its vast green was a place to get lost in as it opened before us like Yankee Stadium. Despite that thrill, we were just little kids too far off base and searching for a corner we could feel safe in, which we did if no one else was around; or better, if other white boys, big ones especially, were already playing. Out we'd go then onto the endless grass to make our diamond: someone's jacket for first, an extra mitt for second, and "that bare spot there, that's third."

What freedom we felt, roaming the center field pasture of Southwest Park, ranging almost forever to pluck a spinning apple out of the air—no cramped back yard, no menacing briars, no windows to shatter. A warning track was in our minds, however, and we knew just where we were, always, and there they were, too, the Negro kids when they came onto the field, as they often did while we were playing. They showed none of our hesitation, however, perhaps because they had no trees to hide behind. The woods were on the east side of the park, our side. Instead, they had a busy street to cross, and maybe they weren't hiding as much inside either, though they were still quite shy and made their own little infield away from us, each group sneaking a peek at the other, equally curious.

They even sounded like us at times: everyone on their side of the field calling "I got it" at once, just as we would, the ball bouncing off their many upturned gloves, just as it did ours. Or someone, black or white, might suddenly holler, "Head's up," because a ball was high in the air, hit hard enough to land between the two groups—their ball like ours, as round and as torn and as smudged by dirt, by touch. And then to throw it back, showing off your arm, no matter its color, and always hearing "thanks" in return, like there was a rule of some kind, like there were baselines that kept both sides at a distance, and together. And afterwards, thirsty, hungry, we'd gather up our dusty gear and head for our earned reward, our boyhood Cooperstown, "The Little Store." How it got that name I have no idea. It *was* small, a one-room area with a soda tank where Cokes and root beers hung on a metal slide in cold water and where ice cream sandwiches lay buried in a freezer box that breathed a mist of ghosts when you opened it. A few grocery items were available too, as I remember, some magazines and papers as well, but who cared, for what waited there in the flag-colored box by the cash register made this neighborhood store for us a place of worship.

No matter our thirst, no matter our hunger, our eyes were on that small cardboard chest with its folded-back top and its treasure of baseball cards in tiny packages smudged with powered sugar and wrapped in red-white-and-blue waxed paper. We'd saved all week for those images of our baseball heroes and had risked the outer reaches of safety in getting there to buy them. We had earned this prize, playing the game of the men we admired, and daring an unknown world to do so. This was our version of the war we heard our fathers talk about over Pabst Blue Ribbon. We, too, had gone behind enemy lines and had earned now the Purple Hearts of pink gum and the hallowed pictures of sluggers in this age of Ike. And unbelievably, here they were again on TV at the end of the century, those very legends we collected—smaller, yes, but only physically, bowing to America on the base paths of Fenway Park.

Although "The Little Store" was in our imaginations the Hall of Fame, it was first and foremost a store, I realize now. It was a business that served two cultures just as baseball around that time was finally starting to do, and as the business of baseball has continued to do, a game today for many peoples. Like the field we often shared, the store fed and watered us, a miniature democracy like the grass of the nearby park, green as the dollars we didn't have. The black ball players my age had about the same amount to spend that my friends and I did, nickels and dimes being our common denominator.

But not so our baseball cards: these we didn't share, but not because of selfishness. My pals and I would often be in the store when the "colored" version of us came in. It didn't matter who arrived first: in ritual fashion, whichever group went immediately to the cooler. Simply to breathe the moist cold from the water in there was wonderful and, often, all any of us could afford. Like us, sometimes they'd split a Coke, or make a loan to one of their teammates, as one of them even did, once upon a time, to our best player, Mike.

We were out of dimes, probably from buying too many cards, so when Mike asked, he must have been overheard in the closeness of the store by the kid in the Brooklyn Dodgers tee shirt with 42 on the sleeve, the tall, skinny, very black guy we always stopped to watch hit. He told Mike he had an extra. I mean, just like that out of nowhere, he said he'd loan Mike a dime. Just like that, as natural as breathing, he spoke to Mike and Mike spoke back, something we seldom did except for that occasional "thanks' at returning a ball or an embarrassed kind of "excuse me" when inside we'd inevitably bump into one another. And so they shook on it to make it official: an I.O.U. from Michael to Jeremiah, a name I'd never heard before. I only knew "Jemima," a name, sadly, we all knew.

Just as we knew "Jackie," and Larry Doby—one Negro to a league. No wonder those black kids didn't care that much about baseball cards. My friends and I would clean out that whole box by the store's register in hopes of finding Stan the Man, as huge as Babe Ruth in our imaginations, but what chance was there of finding a Doby or a Jackie Robinson card in their first years? When Mike tried to settle his loan with a rare and prized Warren Spahn, Jeremiah wasn't interested.

Instead, they agreed on ten sticks of bubble gum, another

common denominator and one we always had plenty of, but

how could he not want the best lefty in baseball, we walked

home wondering.

When Ken Griffey, Jr. shook hands with Ted Williams on

his wheel-chair throne at that 1999 All-Star game, how right it

is that he did so at Fenway Park since the Red Sox were the

last team in baseball to integrate. There wasn't a dry eye in

the house when those two hands met. Even "Teddy

Ballgame" couldn't hold back, that tough old ball-playing

war-hero, that "Splendid Splinter," chewing gum himself as

he was wheeled past the box seats. And here he is again when

I close my eyes, his swaggering grin through the powered

sugar of the card I hold in my hand at "The Little Store."

What a symbol it was, that white haze on each of my heroes,

blurring the picture, sweetening the truth.

"The Little Store" of my boyhood wasn't little at all.

"Something special happened there," whispers Al or Mike,

wherever they are now. Journeying from our block through the nearby woods, then from those sheltering trees to the light of that field, and finally to the store itself, my friends and I crossed a lot more than baselines and brought home more than cards and gum. Our parents had their one-room schoolhouse; this tiny place where everyone thirsted together was ours. From it, we quietly returned with questions about who we were. "Do you think they know they're white?" Jeremiah, like Mike, could have easily asked about us, had there been a tree for him to hide behind.

JUNE TWENTY-FIRST

My mother's cigarette flares and fades,
the steady pulse of a firefly,
on the patio under the chestnut.

The next-door neighbors are over.
My father, still slender, is telling a joke:
laughter jiggles in everyone's drinks.

On his hour's reprieve from sleep,
my little brother dances
in the sprinkler's circle of water.

At fourteen, I'm too old
to run naked with my brother,
too young to laugh with my father.

I stand there with my hands in my pockets.
The sun refuses to set,
bright as a penny in a loafer.

EXTRA INNINGS

The commemorative plaque on the trimmed lawn
of Indian Gap National Cemetery
has "Captain" inscribed before my father's name,
the highest rank among the honored around him,
the other soldiers missing, I presume, in action,
unlike my zany Pop who simply wandered off,
AWOL one spring from the Veteran's Hospital,
his furlough, eternity.

He always marched to an off-beat drummer
and then with Parkinson's
became a wind-up toy soldier who'd charge,
head down from the disease, straight on,
elbowing my mother's vases and crystal
on his way through enemy fire to the end of time.

Wherever he went that day, years ago now,
I see him leading a platoon
of men like those not there around him,
Purple Hearts and heroes, all of them, yes,
but not on this mission with a daffy Captain.

Instead, they've found their way
to some green ballpark,
the 9000th inning about to start
and beer for all forever:
just a bunch of happy ghosts,
waving to the camera.

THE VASE

May in March: our daughter's birthday, somehow now
   twenty
as the crocus uncurl in their black beds, everywhere
yellow, yellow, a whole week of weather
yellow as her hair—

even the bug light on the north porch
where a moth this birthday evening, back too soon,
flaps against the glass flower,
the dust of its wings on the yellow bloom.

In the mild of this scented night, so fragile,
we walk her to her car and back to college:
seat belt on, doors locked, half a carrot cake
in a box beside her and leaning against it the vase

we found and filled with twenty daffodils
to brighten the table tonight, yellow, yellow,
yellow as the petals from its delicate neck
like wishes we'd given light to, gone in a breath.

    --for Amanda Littekin, 1975-1995

THE BLESSED MUTTER OF THE MUSE

"I'm curious: how many others of you were brought up Catholic?" I asked, and to my surprise, ten of the fourteen students in my class at a small Methodist college in Virginia raised their hands.

We'd been discussing a poem submitted by one of them early in the semester, a poem that seemed to this lapsed Catholic to have come out of a similar religious background. There were no obvious references to the Pope or Holy Communion, but the writing had a certain kind of sensibility that struck a chord with me. The young poet had looked at the same scenes I had as a kid, at the Stations of the Cross, no doubt, at its scenes of Jesus' suffering, his writhing face and muscles wrenched in ecstasy and pain.

How could anyone forget those images, especially a child looking up at them in fear and wonder from a hard wooden pew down below? And of equal enduring power were the smells—the indelible, sensual smells of candle-flame, of

"Good strong thick stupefying incense-smoke!" as Robert Browning's dying Bishop utters in his dramatic monologue, "The Bishop Orders His Tomb at Saint Praxed's Church."

This deeply imbedded Catholic sensibility arose specter-like again and again in the four years I worked with young poets at that very Methodist college, Virginia Wesleyan. It was repeated in the many years after at a variety of schools ranging from large, secular public universities to private colleges like VWC. More recently, as the editor of *The Spoon River Poetry Review*, in the thousands of poems that I read in my four-year stint, I could hear Browning's "blessed mutter of the mass" far more often than I thought I might, given contemporary taste.

Sometimes the allusions were obvious, as in these opening lines from "The Calling" by Denise Preston: "Those hands, they make me shy/ cupping the chalice, aloft/ in the stained-glass air./ Does he know their beauty, or were they his crosses—/ too calm for stickball, marbles, war?"

Or the lines might be more subtle like this section from Deirdre Hare Jacobson's "Other Woods": "I breathe in leaf rot and snowmelt,/ savor it as I will the air liquored/with hyacinth, the lilac and peony;/the rose, blooded or pale,/scented with citrus or redolent of wine."

And this troubling, provocative conclusion of "Root and Peril" by Gina Pulciani: "Drought-weary, I'll scrape from my skin/a raw beige for her bone, and I'll bleed her;/you will meet with our marrow right here/on this plain, lengthen in shame along the earth's/mad girth, our common root and peril."

Whether these three poets, or the hundred or more others I published in Spoon River grew up Catholic, I have no idea, but given the images, sound patterns, and sense of mystery so many of them share, I'll bet they did. Could it be then that the muse isn't Greek after all? That Mt. Parnassus is really St. Peter's?

My earliest memories have to do with the rituals of a Sunday morning, the first of which was getting dressed up to go to Church: shoes shined and slacks or dresses ironed, all laid out the night before so we six kids could be ready for the 8 o'clock Mass, a "low" Mass compared to the baroque but lengthy "high" one of 9:30 with its organ music, incense, and the priest's procession down the nave in his golden robe.

Low Mass was shorter and simpler but still replete with mystery. Where else could an ordinary American kid go and hear a foreign language spoken at least once a week, and a dead language at that? Years later in college I chose to spend my junior year in Italy which made no sense because I had studied French since seventh grade. I realize now, however, that Latin was really what I grew up hearing—no, *inhaling*—acted out and chanted as I knelt in prayer those Sunday mornings and every Holy Day.

But Sundays really began on Saturdays, in the haze of late afternoon. At seven years old, the age of reason according to the Church, I would be called in from playing catch with my Protestant friends on the block to go to Confession. From being actually outside, I not only came into the house but had to turn inward as well, to search my soul for my transgressions which weren't that many, at that age anyway. Mostly I made stuff up—saying I'd stolen a water pistol perhaps, or had used a bad word—but I was careful to mention "lying" at the end of my list, figuring that was going to clear my record and make me pure enough for Communion the next morning.

I got quite creative with my sins as I got a little older and started growing hair in odd places. By ten or so, I had myself making out with Patricia Biggins who was the most popular girl in our class, but who, of course, had no interest in me. She was also a foot taller, but that didn't stop me from putting my imaginary lips to hers, though I would have needed a box to stand on to do it. By ending with lying as the last of my sins, I could get away with anything, the way I can with the poems I write.

With their content, at least. I can be most anybody in a poem, the way Robert Browning became a dying Bishop or the murderous Duke of Ferrara in "My Last Duchess." But the patterning and shaping, the writing in syllables, in sounds—these I can't get away from. The rise and fall of the priest's chanting, the repetitions of prayer, the standing, the kneeling, the sitting down: going to Church was a physical experience, visceral and enduring.

It was also scary. I feigned a kind of smart-aleck way of going to Confession because it scared the crap out of me. Waiting there in the pew for others ahead of me, I could feel my pulse in my throat, pounding away. What's taking her so long, my grandmother, a pious old Catholic woman who'd take me with her those Saturdays once in a while. She'd be in there forever, it seemed, though I couldn't imagine what she was confessing. What had she done that week anyway except finish all the ice cream, scoop after scoop of it? I'd close my

eyes and try to pray but saw her spooning away instead,

creamy with joy, indulgently fat, asking God for forgiveness.

   Then it would be my turn and all sugar-plumbs vanished as

I'd draw back the velvety curtain and, trembling, kneel in the

purple light of my side of the confessional, alone now but for

the faint, whispering voice of someone else on the other side,

a grown-up, no doubt, unburdening genuine grown-up sins.

How eternal it was, that wait for the sliding sound of the little

window opening and the shadowy profile of the priest

muttering in mysterious syllables, then suddenly silent.

   "Bless me, Father, for I have sinned," and so I began to

recite the words I'd memorized in Sunday school, words tap-

tap-tapped into me by the nuns, those angels on broom-sticks .

. . "My last confession was a week ago," its perfect iambic

pentameter a subtle mnemonic device, like a line from

Shakespeare, the rise and fall of the beating heart, mine then

in my spondaic throat.

139

For penance, if I hadn't been practicing hyperbole with my lies, I was usually given a light sentence—a couple of "Our Fathers" and a "Hail Mary" which, after decades without saying them, I can still recite without pause. Fear and trembling were part of my motivation for memorizing, no doubt, but the syllables were crafted so you almost couldn't forget: "Our father who art in heaven/Hallowed be thy name./Thy kingdom come/Thy will be done/On earth as it is in heaven." With all that repetition, rhyme (both exact and slant), plus a basic iambic pattern, the words of my penance were a lot easier to memorize than any poem in today's *New Yorker,* which I defy anyone to do. Plus, the prayers came with pictures like those of the "Stations of the Cross." Little did I know it at the time, but I was learning to see in symbols, ones that would never leave me.

In *The Art of Memory,* Frances Yates explains how classical orators could deliver speeches hours long without any notes. They trained their minds to map ideas or facts onto virtual loci they created as mnemonic devices. The artificial place—such as a room in a house and the hall leading to it— became identified with the concept to be remembered. The more "active" the scene, the more memorable it was. Thus, blood stains, purple cloaks, and crowns helped the orator remember "by arousing emotional effects," as Yates put it.

When I first discovered this book in graduate school, I was flabbergasted. So, the Church fathers knew very well what they were doing when they created the "Stations" with specific locations along the north and south walls leading to the altar in the east. And as for blood stains and other emotional magnets, each locus was a sensual plethora of spirit and flesh.

And I not only saw purple in the "Stations" and trembled in its failing light in the Confessional, I lived it at Lent, that forty-day period of Christ's suffering when even my grandmother tried to give up "her cream," as she liked to call it. She went to confession a lot, it seemed, during those days of sacrifice, a spooky time because all the statues were cloaked in twilight—even my favorite, St. Francis, who looked like my pious and gentle grandfather, though Grampy was the guy who smuggled in dear Nana's frozen goodies.

But on Easter morning, the place was ablaze with color, the altar festooned in flowers, *yellow, yellow*, and the priest's robe adazzle of gold—dark to light, mourning to joy: symbols so simple and profound. My earliest memories are of these purposeful moments that transcended language, whether living or dead.

And then to Holy Communion!—me with my slicked-down, schoolboy hair, all dressed up and sinless, going down the aisle through the wafting smoke of the candles to kneel at the altar: "Dominus vobiscum . . . In spirito tuo," the priest coming near, cupping the chalice, the bread now body, the wine its blood, that wafer on my tongue a holy metaphor, the Son of God Himself.

Who wouldn't write poems after all that!?

In his essay, "Milktongue, Goatfoot, Twinbird," Donald Hall reminds us of the primitive origins of poetry: the newborn's babbling and kicking, and those two tiny hands in flight. Anyone who has raised a child or has been around an infant knows this world of the crib, an instinctual world where the primal elements of lyric poetry are rediscovered by each of us. "Milktongue": the play with sounds and succulent pleasure in the mouth, the source of vowels and consonants; "Goatfoot": the muscularity of fitful legs always in motion, the genesis of rhythm; "Twinbird," the two lonely hands seeking each other, our bisymmetry the origin of pattern, of rhyme, of love.

Lying on his death-bed in St. Praxed's Church, Browning's old Bishop would seem a long way from the crib, but not so. Describing the marble he wants for his tomb, the tongue in his mouth is still lush with pleasure: "Peach-blossom marble all, the rare, the ripe/As fresh poured red wine of a mighty pulse." His muscular energy, his "kicking" like Hall's "Goatfoot," is transformed by age to a rant at his "sons": "There, leave me!/For ye have stabbed me with ingratitude/To death—ye wish it—God, ye wish it! Stone/—Gritstone, a crumble!" And all the while, hypocrite though he is, the dying Bishop longs to retrieve the part of him that's missing, that "twinbird" hand of the infant, that longed-for "other": "Nephews—sons mine . . . ah God, I know not!/Well—She, men, would have to be your mother once,/Old Gandolf envied me, so fair she was!"

No wonder Christmas and Easter are Catholicism's greatest celebrations: from the sky-blue of the Madonna's robe and sun-gold of her halo, to the blood-stained garments of Jesus and the purple shrouds on the saints at Lent, to the burst of silver and sunlight forty days later, Easter Sunday. Buried below the troubled *institution* of the Church lie archetypes as deeply human as those of the crib.

Although I haven't been to Mass regularly in years, my senses remain tuned to its sounds and symbols when I read a poem or when I try to write one. The altar was bare back in the chapel of that Methodist college years ago, and its plaster statues prosaic, without a trace of anguish or joy, or as I came to realize, of both. Both at once, that is—the anguish, the joy, like the spirit and the flesh, inseparable—that profound truth made memorable by the colors around me as a boy in that huge pew, by those stupefying smells and that rhythmic chanting that haunt me still, and will forever, amen.

MILK

When I was a boy
there was music to milk in the morning,
its windy ring, the bottles clinking
like chimes in the dark
when I'd wake before school
to hear the milkman bringing
on his white wings our milk
thick with cream for the licking.

From the tin box on the back stoop
I'd lift them slippery as fish still dripping
cool against my small boy's chest, hugging
glass to the white, icebox door,
my morning chore before the nuns,
those angels on broom-sticks over me hovering
asking why, *why God made thee*,
their steel-rimmed eyes and me, still yawning.

Milk, oh milk, sweet, sweet milk,
it melts a winter morning
this milk I warm for my kids, this soothing
silk from the carton with its faces now
of the missing, vague in wax, everybody's children
who late for the school bell's ringing
took a ride one day forever.
The bus, kids, it's here. I love you, get going.

SMOKE

From his window on the ward
I watch it puff from the hospital stack,
black and billowing,
vanishing far across the fields,

and wonder is it coal or oil
thickening the thin fall air.
Five floors up, I'm glad for glass
and wind that blows the stench away

though in the seasonless ether of this place
I crave the smell of burning leaves,
to sit again on the damp, raked grass
and watch my father cupping a match.

He is kneeling to the leaves,
the reds, the yellows, the orange leaves,
the smoke in whispers first
soon full with the breath of fall,

the rhythm of his arms and rake
ghostlike through the gray.
Then, in the swirling haze, he disappears,
slips away to circle back

where I'm waiting there afraid,
searching the smoke for my father—
a hide-and-seek he liked to play
every fall the same, sneaking up behind me

from where he was hiding,
coming back always, like some kind of magic
a boy could believe, from nowhere,
like a promise he would never die.

OCTOBER

Today, they're cutting the corn,
the stalks dry and blowing, brown
and rattling, rattling
when you walk by
as if something were inside,
a deer, a coon, something
alive, someone maybe.
But today
they're cutting it down
as they do every October,
the combines on the back roads,
on the fields,
working all night, next day and next,
until the land is flat again
and we can see
some ranch house we forgot
a mile or so away.
Out here
the corn is a special mystery,
a haunted place
where children warned not to
want to play.
No wonder each September
before the harvest
some farm kid disappears,
losing himself in the tall acres,
tunneling under the sabers
rattling over his head,
vanishes for hours, for days.
Usually, they come back
or are found; once in a while,
they're not. That's why
slowing to a walk

somewhere out from home
and out of breath,
I always stop, sure I've heard
something in there,
something I woke jogging by,
one of those kids maybe
in the forest of corn,
hear him, the closer I get,
running away.

BUSING TO BYZANTIUM

A couple of springs ago, my daughter and I took a bus from Thessaloniki in northern Greece over the mountains to Istanbul. The trip was ghastly. In an effort to save some money, I'd found us seats on a local—a big mistake. Despite the promise from the ticket vendor that no smoking was allowed, everyone (including the driver) lit up as soon as we left the station. Twelve hours of unbreathable air, together with the bus stereo turned to its highest decibel with cheap *bouzouki* music, meant a long night. Fortunately, I'd brought along plenty to read, including a copy of William Butler Yeats' great poem about his longed-for journey to this same city, but even he could never have imagined the "Fish, flesh, or fowl" of that fumy bus. How my sixteen-year-old daughter slept through it all, I'll never know.

We arrived in dawn's early smog. My stomach hurt from tension, though hardly as much as it would a little later from the melting ice in a Coke I drank, try as I might not to drink the water those cubes were made of. I'd also never heard the prayer service from a minaret before, and when I did at 5:00 AM while trying to hail a cab, I thought we'd landed in the middle of a revolution. I was unnerved by the exotic cry. This was my first visit to a Muslim country, and though I'd read about what to expect, the abstract never matches the actual when traveling.

There was our taxi ride, for example. Coughing and inhaling at the same time, the driver squinted through the blue haze from his cigarette at our hotel voucher and nodded knowingly. "See, Dad, everything's going to be all right," said my yawning daughter, dismayed at my distress. She curled up in the back while I doubled up with belly cramps in the front, the authoritative male tourist's place next to the driver. I'd make sure he took us there directly, wherever *there* was. All I knew was that we were heading east, the rising sun a mock harvest moon through the opaque air.

The bus terminal was apparently well west of town, or so our driver made it seem as his beat-up Fiat banged along, hitting every pot-hole he could find, and there were plenty. "This is no cab ride for old men," I whispered to Yeats, especially if they wear dentures—or had, as I did, an immediate need for the bathroom. But off in the distance, there was hope (of an aesthetic kind at least): I could see a couple of ships on what must have been the Bosphorus, and, in front of them as we grew closer to the city, the silhouetted domes of the first mosques I'd ever seen.

"Look at how the light's behind them, Meg—how they look like they have halos." My poetry, however, went unheard—by my daughter anyway, who was out cold. The cabby, however, nodded once again as if I'd given him directions and squealed the wheels sharply left, which, for a moment, had to be north but soon became a thousand-and-one tiny streets and intricate alleys. A Topkapi's worth of Turkish lira later, we pulled in front of the third hotel with the same name as the one I had booked, but this time it was actually ours.

Over the next three days we received the usual attention a visitor attracts in Istanbul, especially one with a lovely young daughter along. Even small boys had their own business cards and tried to sell us everything from carpets and clothes to whirling-dervish spinning tops, the latter about how I felt by the end of each day. No matter where we went, youthful men would trail us around, offering to be our guides, but I suspect more interested in my dollars or my daughter than improving their English. "Hey, honey, remember me from Honolulu?" we'd hear, wandering the endless and famous bazaar, its maze of pathways glistening with trinkets, aglow with false gold.

It took Meg little time to realize she was outnumbered. Where are the women, she wanted to know, or the girls her own age? We saw very few as we wandered about, and when we did, their faces and hair were always covered. "Not a good place to buy lipstick," she concluded, half laughing but a little scared, too. Even with her long yellow locks tied in a bun and blue jeans changed for a shapeless skirt, I could have returned home with any number of camels in trade.

From both exhaustion and timidity, we didn't go out at night and spent the evenings in the hotel bar with the other tourists who gathered there for the same reasons. Mostly from Germany and Japan, but from India and South Africa as well, everyone in varieties of English told much the same story: Istanbul is a fascinating city but quit trying to sell us something. It seemed that lipstick was about the only thing *not* for sale.

The bottle of Budweiser in front of me and the McDonald's just down the street led me to thinking that the ambitious people of this city were not the only capitalists around, ardent as they were. I was at the end of a year's appointment as a Fulbright professor in Greece and had seen plenty of evidence of aggressive sales there as well. It's hard to walk through the Plaka in Athens and not come out the other side with something shiny in your otherwise empty pocket.

154

The history of trade is as deep there as it is here in Turkey, a common bond for these ancient enemies. In fact, most of the Greeks on that awful bus trip had come to Istanbul to shop, and come to think of it, I'd also bargained our route east. Laying down your weapons to pick up your packages has become the contemporary way of making peace, as nations have given way to corporations. Maybe there *are* no nations anymore, and all we care about is buying and selling. The sovereign State of Nike. The independent Country of Coke. And here in Istanbul the kids start early, like that little boy this morning, that eight-year-old who spoke perfect English, the child we thought was so cute. He was hawking his small carpets right outside the Suliman Mosque, wasn't he? Right in its shadow.

Those evenings in the bar nursing a brew gave me the chance to ruminate and to skim over guidebooks and histories. No doubt, the kind of commercialism we'd all been experiencing was part of Istanbul's great past and had been since the Bosphorus first flowed between the Sea of Marmara

155

and the Black, and that's a long time. But so, too, had the life of the spirit been the center of this crossroad of faiths, and I was beginning to wonder where the sense of worship had gone. Those timeless eyes in the gold mosaics of Hagia Sophia: could they be found anywhere outside that once-holy sphere, itself now neither cathedral nor mosque but a pay-as-you-enter museum? And the silent poetry of the Blue Mosque's lyrical designs? It was quickly gone when we stepped from that holy quiet into the honking of taxis and hoots of horny men. Where was the spirit of this eternal city? Where was its soul? The answer, my friend, was blowin' in the wind.

At the bar each night was a singer who came on for an hour or so, strumming a guitar and singing Bob Dylan songs but with a sweeter voice than Bobby Zimmerman ever had, once or now. A son of the sixties myself, I was at first amused, then gradually taken in; my daughter, part of the new Grateful Dead generation, was enthralled. No one else in the place paid any attention, chatting away the whole time he

156

sang, but Meg and I knew the tunes and crooned along quietly. The young singer never looked our way, however, though with our obvious interest and our being the only Americans in the small crowd, I thought he might, the way we Americans manage to find one another wherever we go, like it or not. Apparently, he didn't like it, since he never made eye contact with us until our last night in Turkey.

Once again, my daughter and I were the only ones who clapped, and after he'd set down his guitar and unleashed his harmonica, he took a small package from under his seat and headed our way. All kinds of thoughts went through my head. He looks like a college kid; I wonder where? Maybe he wants to share some carpet stories, talk American to American. Let me guess his name--he looks more like a Robert than a Bob; not quite as bubbly. But he didn't say a word, or sing one either. He barely looked at us as he handed me the package. I asked him if he'd like to have a beer—they even have "Bud Light," I said—but he didn't respond. He hardly understood, in fact, and well he couldn't.

157

This Bob Dylan didn't speak English. Oh maybe a word or two—"geeft," he kept mumbling, "geeft"—but as we found out later, he'd memorized the lyrics of all the songs he sang so well and had little idea what they meant. Somehow, "The Times They Are A-Changin'" and "Blowing in the Wind" had a meaning that he sensed rather than actually understood, the way a child learns gesture and tone long before definition. And indeed, he stood before us like a child, the first shy one we'd seen in Istanbul.

He kept pointing towards the package wrapped in a paper bag. "I think he wants you to open it," Megan said, as bewildered by his silence as I, and expecting what I did: yet another thing to buy. I opened it anyway, only to find one of the loveliest gifts I've ever been given: in pastel pinks and blues, before our eyes was a water-color of a mosque at sunrise, shimmering in the early light like a vision. And on the Bosphorus in the foreground, a delicate sailboat, silent through the lapping waves, its two stick-figure passengers on their quiet way to the Black Sea perhaps or, like my daughter and me, back to Greece, or wherever home happened to be. "Geeft," was all he said and wouldn't take a penny or even the actual lira I offered him, which made me ashamed of myself the moment I did.

He painted it himself, the fluent clerk explained as we were checking out. He had even framed it, and despite the horrible ride back to Thessaloniki—poor Megan had the melted ice cubes distress this direction—I felt a wholeness inside the many times I took it out in the sooty bus. He was aware of us the entire time, I realized. I guess he was grateful that someone heard his voice, had paid attention to the songs that must have taken so long for him to learn. But what a jerk I am, I kept thinking, trying to pay him. I'm as programmed as everyone else.

The painting hangs in my house as I write this, a treasure without a price—a moment, that is, but one that nonetheless sings "of what is past, or passing, or to come," as Yeats has sung about the city's "Monuments of unaging intellect." But the lyrics of this painted song are far more simple: no "gold

159

enameling," just little watery lines of color. When my own

check book and credit cards and those voices on the phone

trying to sell me something make me feel like a cash machine,

I look up at this paper mosaic and sail away, "To the holy city

of Byzantium."

TIMETABLE

Behind me this morning on the train,
in the early light made warm
through the window's double-glass,
an old Amish man,
the rough of his beard gone white,
is singing to his wife, both of them
round and red-faced as apples
in their simple clothes, bonnet and hat,
their seat on the Amtrak
one of those looking south
as we head north to Chicago.

My back against theirs,
I close my eyes to listen
but in the privacy of their language,
in the seclusion of their ways,
I can't make out the words
and hear instead the rails,
their heartbeat like hooves
as he hums to her in the sun,
one hand I dream in hers—the other, the reins,
their buggy's glass lamp swinging in time
towards their farm in Arthur.

Suddenly awake, suddenly alive,
feeling suddenly happier than I have in months,
I want to call them you and me,
to sing to you in words
some guy going to a meeting in the city
can't understand.
And oh, if I could hold your hand
just like that,
no one else on the train,
just the two of us in our buggy,
looking back.

161

FOR MY WIFE, CUTTING MY HAIR

You move around me expertly like the good, round
Italian barber I went to in Florence
years before we met, his scissors
a razor he sharpened on a belt.

But at first when you were learning, I feared
for my neck, saw my ears like sliced fruit
on the newspapered floor. Taking us back in time,
you cleverly clipped my head in a flat-top.

The years in between were styles no one had ever seen,
or should see again: when the wind rose
half my hair floated off in feathers,
the other half bristling, brief as a brush.

In the chair, almost asleep, I hear the bright
scissors dancing. Hear you hum, full-breasted as Aida,
carefully trimming the white from my temples,
so no one, not even I, will know.

RIGHT ON

Each Spring
like two old ducks
my ninety-year-old grandparents
wing their way on the Interstate
from Florida to Maine,
never breaking 50
in their '49 Chevy,
cruising inexorably
in the left-hand-lane.

ABOUT THE AUTHOR

Bruce Guernsey, a native New Englander, is Distinguished Professor Emeritus at Eastern Illinois University where he taught for twenty-five years. He was awarded seven faculty excellence-in-teaching awards, and in 1992-93 was selected as the State of Illinois Board of Governors' "Professor of the Year," the highest award in that state system. He has also taught at William and Mary, Johns Hopkins, and Virginia Wesleyan College where he was Poet in Residence for four years.

His poems have appeared in *Poetry, The Atlantic, The American Scholar,* and many of the quarterlies. His essays have found a home over the years in such journals as *The Virginia Quarterly, War, Literature and the Arts, Dappled Things,* and *Chronicles.* He is a former Editor of *The Spoon River Poetry Review.* Several of his poems have been featured in *American Life in Poetry* edited by former Poet Laureate, Ted Kooser.

The recipient of Fellowships from the NEA, The MacDowell Colony, Bread Loaf, and the Illinois Arts Council, Guernsey has been honored with two Fulbright Senior Lectureships in American Poetry to Portugal and Greece. He has also twice sailed around the world as a faculty member with Semester at Sea.

Made in the USA
Columbia, SC
09 November 2021

48558379R00095